MESOPOTAMI
(1919-1924)

THE STORY OF AN I
WITH
THE BRITISH ARMY OF OᴄᴄU...

Volume 4
of
THE COLOURFUL LIFE OF AN ENGINEER
Memoirs of Harry Chickall Lott MC

As Peter Scott wrote of himself, in his autobiography:
"I am, without question, the luckiest, and I believe, the happiest man I know."

Grosvenor House
Publishing Limited

The right of John Brian Lott to be identified as the author of this
work has been asserted in accordance with Section 78
of the Copyright, Designs and Patents Act 1988

The book cover is copyright to John Brian Lott

This book is published by
Grosvenor House Publishing Ltd
Link House
140 The Broadway, Tolworth, Surrey, KT6 7HT.
www.grosvenorhousepublishing.co.uk

A CIP record for this book
is available from the British Library

ISBN 978-1-83975-478-4

About the Author

Harry was born in 1883, a descendant of the Lott family who, for 200 years, had farmed at the Valley Farm and Willy Lott's Cottage in Flatford, made famous by Constable's paintings. In 1890 his father left farming and invested in a foundry business, Lott & Walne, in Dorchester where Harry attended Dorchester Grammar School and won a scholarship to study Electrical Engineering at the Central Technical College in London.

He first saw Canada on an Atlantic cable laying expedition in 1905 and emigrated there in 1907, where he worked as an inspector on the construction of bridges, buildings, and hydro-electric schemes in five provinces, living in Montreal, Toronto and Winnipeg and in construction camps in the backwoods of Manitoba.

Harry returned to England in 1914 to join up for WWI and served in the trenches with the 8th Royal Sussex Pioneer Regiment. He was awarded the Military Cross for acts of exemplary bravery and promoted to the rank of Major after the battles of the Somme and Passchendaele where he was wounded. He was transferred to the Royal Engineers and, after the clearance of the battlefields in 1919, he was posted to the British Army of Occupation in Mesopotamia where he was appointed Lieutenant Colonel in charge of Mechanical & Electrical Services in Baghdad and Basra.

When he was demobilized in 1924 Harry sailed from Basra to Bombay where he joined the Empress of Canada's first round-the-world cruise to Vancouver and returned home from Montreal after visiting friends and relatives across Canada.

He joined Balfour Beatty Co. Ltd. in London for whom he worked as a consulting engineer for 30 years until he retired aged 72 in 1955. In the 1920's and 30's he carried out surveys for hydro-electric schemes for the East African Power and Lighting Company in Kenya, undertook assignments in India and Nigeria as well as another round-the-world trip beginning with a journey to China on the Trans-Siberian Railway to submit a bid for the Shanghai Municipal Electricity Department.

His memoirs describe a remarkable life full of adventure and good luck. He did not marry until he was 59 and had a son Brian who has edited these memoirs, adding some historical background and other items of interest from the diaries which Harry kept from 1900 until he died in 1975 aged 91.

Preface

These memoirs were originally written, or rather typed using an old-fashioned Smith-Corona typewriter, by my father, Harry Lott during his retirement from the late 1950's until a year before he died aged 91 in May 1975. He had kept daily diaries from 1900 until a week or so before his death, as well as numerous personal papers, photographs, menus, cuttings, reports, and letters. These provided source material for the several volumes of memoirs he wrote covering his first 50 years, up to the mid-1930's, when he considered that the 'colourful' years of his life had come to an end. By then he had become somewhat frustrated that his company, Balfour Beatty, no longer sent him on interesting overseas assignments but instead kept him office bound in London, using his extensive international experience and engineering judgement to evaluate and comment on the various new projects and business opportunities which came their way.

Having essentially completed his memoirs he asked a writer and journalist, Peter Ford, for his opinion on their suitability for publication. Peter thought that they were full of interest and suggested that they would benefit from the inclusion of more personal comments on the various individuals mentioned and that some links to current events of the day would add context. As a consequence my father added many inserts into the text and extra pages of anecdotes and detail wherever he could, with the result that, without the benefit of a word processor, the memoirs became even more like a scrap-book which no-one would ever read.

I inherited his memoirs, 75 years of his diaries and a filing cabinet full of his papers, photograph albums and other memorabilia. Whilst sorting through all these documents for archiving or disposal I decided to edit his memoirs, put them on a word processor and prepare them for publication in the hope that they may be of interest to future generations. During this process I added some extra material from my father's diaries and personal papers and I also inserted some historical background details in places, however, the majority of the content is exactly as he wrote it.

In preparing these memoirs for publication I decided to split them into five separate volumes, each dealing with a different chapter of my father's life. All five parts, if published together, would result in a book of a size which would put off most readers. If edited to remove many of the details, then each part would be of less interest to anyone reading it as a historical document. I can imagine my children, grand-children and possibly their descendants being interested in picking up a particular volume on, say, Canada, Mesopotamia or World War I and reading that, whilst not being prepared to tackle all five volumes at any one time.

The second reason is that, outside the family, each volume has potentially a quite different readership. Some readers or historical researchers may be interested in one or two of the volumes but not in all of them. The following summary of the contents of each volume provides an over view of the memoirs as a whole and enables readers to determine their interest or otherwise in the other volumes.

My father was an engineer, an officer and always a gentleman. He had a remarkable life and an interesting and varied international career in engineering during the first 30 years of the 20th Century. After 59 years of independence as a bachelor, he married my mother in 1942 and they enjoyed 32 years of very happily married life. In his last three decades he was a wise and wonderful father to me, despite being 60 years my senior.

This work is my tribute to him. It has been a real pleasure re-living his experiences, researching stories of the people he met, the places he visited and the engineering history he describes. I hope that it will be of some interest and inspiration to my family, his descendants, and future generations of engineers.

J Brian Lott OBE
London, 2020

Acknowledgements

In researching the historical background to this volume I have referred to the following books from which I have included a few quotations in the text in italics. Google has also been a useful source of some additional facts about the places my father visited and the people he met.

Wilfred Thesiger	The Marsh Arabs
Wilfred Thesiger	Arabian Sands
Janet Wallach	Desert Queen - The Extraordinary Life of Gertrude Bell
James Barr	A Line in the Sand - Britain, France and the Struggle that shaped the Middle East
Doris Lessing	Under My Skin - Autobiography
Bernard Lewis	The Middle East

The Colourful Life of an Engineer
Volumes 1 to 5

Contents

The Colourful Life of an Engineer

Volume 4

Mesopotamia
(1919 – 1924)

The Story of an Engineer
with
The British Army of Occupation

Introduction

My four years with the British Army of Occupation in Mesopotamia after the War were a welcome contrast to the previous four years which I had spent in the trenches and battlefields of France and Belgium.

I arrived in Basra on 5th November 1919 via Bombay, thirty-six days after leaving Southampton, and sailed up the Tigris to Baghdad where I was based for the next 2 years. My appointment as Assistant Director of Works and Director of Electrical and Mechanical (E&M) Services with the Mesopotamian Expeditionary Force came with a promotion to the rank of Lieutenant Colonel.

Besides a team of Army officers, all engineers, I also had about 8,000 men, mostly Arab, Persian and Baghdadi Jewish civilians, under my administration as well as some enrolled Indians from the Indian Army including Hindus, Muslims, Sikhs, and Punjabis whom we employed as electricians, mechanics and wiremen, clerks and store-keepers.

In 1922 I was transferred to Basra as Deputy Director of RE Services and spent the next two years working with the RAF there, managing projects, including the construction of their new base and hospital at Hinaidi, and their HQ, barracks, hospital, and rest camp in Basra, in addition to our regular work of maintaining the electricity and water supplies and ice works in the region.

However, before describing my life in Mesopotamia, it is worth summarising my background and adventures before 1919 for those who have not read Volumes 1, 2 and 3 of my memoirs. In the first volume I began with my family origins, visits to the Valley Farm at Flatford and Willy Lott's Cottage where my ancestors had been yeoman farmers for 200 years, and I described our way of life in a typical East Anglian farmhouse in late Victorian England, almost 150 years ago.

Following the agricultural depression of the 1880s, my father left farming and moved to Dorchester in 1890, where he invested in a partnership in an iron foundry business, Lott & Walne, which he thought would be more profitable than farming. So my schooldays were spent at Dorchester Grammar school, and my interest in nature developed on field trips in the area with my school friend (later Dr) Cyril Day who became a noted naturalist. I was also musical, and, like my sisters, was taught to play the piano at an early age. This led to my appointment at the age of 15 as organist at our local church, a position I held until just after Queen Victoria died in 1901, when I obtained a scholarship to study Electrical Engineering at the Central Technical College in London, later to become part of London University.

I spent three years in digs and at college in London, from 1901 to 1904, at a time when many new and exciting engineering developments were taking place, the first steam cars and omnibuses were replacing horse-drawn carriages, and the first underground railway, the Twopenny Tube, had recently opened.

My first real engineering job, working for a firm of consulting engineers, was as an assistant engineer on the Atlantic cable laying expedition in 1905. During that trip, whilst our ship was being repaired in Halifax, Nova Scotia, I made a brief visit to Quebec City, Montreal, Toronto and Niagara Falls, and fell in love with Canada. It was a young country full of opportunity, and I decided that I would return, but before doing so I needed to obtain more practical experience as an electrical engineer, which I did during 18 months in the workshops of Marshall's of Gainsborough. Having obtained my father's permission to emigrate, I left Liverpool on the SS Victorian in July 1907, aged 24, and my experiences in Canada are the subject of Volume 2.

I landed in Montreal, along with many other young immigrants, with only £10 in my pocket and no job to go to. Within a week I was working for the Allis Chalmers Bullock Company in their high-tension electrical testing department for 15 cents/hr. After 6 weeks I moved to a better job with the Canadian Inspection Company, for whom I worked as an inspector of steelwork and bridge construction in Montreal, New Glasgow (NS), and St Casimir (PQ), before being sent to Winnipeg (MB) to supervise the erection of a bridge over the Red River.

Descriptions of my work as an engineer, and life in lodgings in Montreal during that first winter, and subsequently in Winnipeg, making new friends, ice-skating, snow-shoeing, skiing, and exploring my new surroundings, provide a glimpse of life during those early days in Canada before the War. After my next assignment in Toronto, inspecting the manufacture of a Caméré curtain dam, I returned to England for my first home leave in May 1909.

Back in Canada in August, I began a two-year assignment for Smith, Kerry and Chace, consulting engineers, working as an inspector on the construction of a 77 mile long transmission line between Winnipeg and the new hydro-electric power plant being built at Pointe du Bois. The following two years, most of which were spent in construction camps in the backwoods north-east of Winnipeg, were some of the most colourful of my life. I lived in a tent during the harsh winters, when the temperature fell to 40 degrees below zero, and during the hot, midge-infested summers when the mercury rose to 100 degrees Fahrenheit. Occasional visits to civilisation in Winnipeg to meet friends provided a welcome contrast to the rough conditions of camp life.

During weekends I went on canoe trips on Lac du Bonnet and on the Winnipeg River with friends, and on hunting expeditions for moose and caribou with Arthur Mitchell, a well-known local character, as a guide.

After Winnipeg I spent three months near Prince Albert, supervising drilling work in the bed of the North Saskatchewan River, to find a suitable location for a new hydro-electric dam to serve the city. We did not encounter bed-rock and advised against the construction of a dam, but the city engineers, ignoring our advice, went ahead, leaving Prince Albert with massive debts and the La Colle Falls dam half-finished a few years later.

Then, after a second visit to England to see my family, I returned accompanied by Cyril Skinner, whose mother had employed me to 'show him Canada' and help him find a job there. Having done that, I started work with T. Pringle & Son, consulting engineers in Montreal, and was sent to survey the site for a hydro-electric scheme on the St Maurice River, near Grand-Piles. This was followed by design work in the Montreal office for several new buildings, and finally my appointment as Chief Designer of Kodak's large new factory in Toronto, to be built in reinforced concrete, in the early days of that form of construction.

When war broke out in Europe I joined the local Company of the Westmount Rifles and started training with them in the evenings. However, there seemed little prospect of an early commission and of going to France, so, in December 1914, I threw up my job and paid my passage back to England to join up there. My experiences in the War are the subject of Volume 3 of my memoirs.

I joined the 8th Battalion of the Royal Sussex (Pioneer) Regiment, and had four months training in Colchester and on Salisbury Plain, before we were sent to France in July 1915. As a 2nd Lieutenant I had charge of a platoon of 40 'Pioneers' whose main work was digging trenches and dugouts, and building shelters and barricades.

My war memoirs cover some of the major battles, including the Somme in 1916/17 and Passchendaele in 1917, where I was wounded, but do not describe the military strategy and tactics in any detail. They focus instead on the everyday life of the officers and men in my Pioneer Battalion, and later in the Royal Engineers, when I was appointed Forward Area Officer in the 5th Army Headquarters, in charge of the tramways and light railways required to deliver supplies and ammunition to the troops at the front.

The diary notes which I wrote at the time in billets and dugouts near the front line, were sent home as my letters for passing round the family. We were not allowed to include any strategically important information, even place names had to be omitted, so in writing the memoirs I added short extracts from other sources to provide historical background and continuity where necessary.

Promotion came quickly as senior officers fell and those below took over command. By the end of the War I had been promoted from 2nd Lieutenant to Captain in the 8th Royal Sussex Regiment, and then to Major in the Royal Engineers. I was Mentioned in Despatches three times, and awarded the Military Cross in January 1917. The fact that I escaped serious injury for more than two years, until October 1917, despite numerous near misses, testifies to my extreme luck. Even when I was wounded, I was lucky that it was not so serious as to affect my future health and career.

Soon after the Armistice in November 1918, I and several of my colleagues caught Spanish Flu'; I spent three weeks in hospitals in Lille and Étaples before being sent to convalesce in the luxury of the Grand Hotel du Cap Martin, not far from Nice. When I returned to the battlefields in February 1919, I joined the Headquarters staff of the Royal Engineers at Loos, a suburb of Lille, as Senior Construction Engineer managing the clearance of the battle areas. I remained in that role until September, when I was told that my engineering experience was required in Mesopotamia, where I was to join the British Army of Occupation in Baghdad. That was to be my next adventure and is the subject of this Volume 4 of my memoirs.

My work in Mesopotamia was to look after the existing electricity generating, water supply and refrigeration facilities, and construct new ones to service British garrisons and the local population in an area 800 miles from east to west and 300 miles north to south around Baghdad. During my inspection visits to our various units, I travelled by car across the desert for shorter trips, and by train overnight for longer ones, and became familiar will all the towns from Mosul, Kirkuk and Tekrit in the north, to Hillah and Dewaniyeh on the Euphrates, and to Kut and Amara on the Tigris in the south.

For Christmas that first year I visited our Persian lines of communication and Kermanshah, where I stayed with Alfred and Emily Maude Tayler. Alfred was a cousin of mine from East Anglia, who had lost a leg in the War, and married his Irish nurse. He joined a bank which sent him to a branch in Kermanshah where their daughter Doris (Lessing), the Nobel prize-winning author, was born.

The Arab Revolt in 1920 caused us a great deal of anxiety and expense, reinforcing our units to ensure their safety. Baghdad in summer was oppressive, and the Arab unrest at the delays to their independence had boiled over in the 100 degree heat.

My daily life in Baghdad was a mixture of early rising and hard work during the day, followed by relaxed evenings in our mess, 'The Work House' as we called it, on River Street. Guest nights sometimes included the ladies, officers' wives and nurses from the military and civil hospitals. During autumn weekends we enjoyed shooting trips for duck on the river, or for sand-grouse and partridges in the desert.

After I transferred to Basra in January 1922, my main role was to maintain the power, water and ice-making facilities, and complete our projects for the RAF, whilst reducing our establishment to a fraction of the initial number, in line with Government policy of cutting the cost of the British presence in the region.

Feisal was appointed King of Iraq in 1921, and I attended three dinners with him in June 1923, when he paid his first official visit to his Southern Province to meet local officials in Basra.

Visits to Ur of the Chaldees, shooting trips in the Marshes, tennis parties at the Makina Club, becoming a Freemason, and other social events, added variety to the rather less comfortable life in the heat and humidity of the south. Towards the end of my time in Basra, I used to fly in a two-seater RAF de Havilland DH 9A to make regular inspection visits to Nasiriyeh. At that time I was working with Air Marshall Sir John Salmond who thanked me for staying on an extra 12 months at his request to continue the work of reducing the staff numbers, before leaving the country to resume my civilian career.

I was given a wonderful Farewell Dinner at the Makina Club and a Garden Party which were fully reported in the Times of Mesopotamia on 23rd February 1924, when I left Basra on the SS Vasna, bound for Bombay. In Bombay, I was lucky to obtain a berth on the Empress of Canada on its round-the-world cruise to Vancouver. From there I crossed Canada looking up friends and relatives on the way, before returning home from Montreal. This trip, and my subsequent world travels, and life in London between the Wars, are the subject of Volume 5.

Harry C. Lott

Mesopotamia
(1919-1924)
The Story of an Engineer with the British Army of Occupation

Transfer to Mesopotamia in 1919

I was 36 when I left France on 4th August 1919, almost exactly 4 years after I had landed there with the 8th Royal Sussex Pioneers in 1915. The War Office had decided to send me to Mesopotamia because of my engineering experience. After about six weeks in England, which I spent mostly at Wenham with my parents, on 23rd September I received orders to sail from Southampton four days later, en route to Baghdad. So began the next chapter in my life which lasted four and a half years, until February 1924, when I was finally demobilised and returned to civilian life.

Mesopotamia had become of critical importance to the British Empire because of its oil, without which the Allies could not have won the war. In 1911 Churchill, then First Lord of the Admiralty, had ordered a major change, switching the British Navy's battleships from coal burning engines to oil. The new developments in motorcar and aircraft technology would also ensure that oil became the future source of power for the world. Britain had been the world's leading supplier of coal but had no oil of her own. In 1912 Churchill signed an agreement for a major share in the Anglo-Persian Oil Company (from which BP developed), with its oil wells in southern Persia and refineries at Abadan, close to Basra.

The oil-fields of southern Persia, now under British control, were the most inexhaustible proven fields in the world; the Mosul province and the banks of the mid-Euphrates promised to produce oil in great quantities although the full extent of the fields was not then known.

Britain's war on the Eastern Front had begun with the battle at Gallipoli to cut off the Turkish forces on their way to Baghdad. Britain's strategic objective throughout the war in the Middle East had been to take advantage of the disintegration of the Ottoman Empire to unite the Arabs against the Turks and stave off the Turks before they could make two serious strikes; one at Egypt and the Suez Canal, and the other at Mesopotamia and the oil refineries on the Persian Gulf.

The maintenance of Britain's trade route to India was also of critical importance against the threat from the Germans, who had assisted the Turks in financing and constructing an important railway line from Berlin to Baghdad. The capture of Baghdad by British troops on 10th March 1917 had consolidated Britain's authority in the area. When the war ended, the British retained responsibility for the administration of the region until it was properly handed over to newly created Arab governments.

The Paris Peace Conference, where the leaders of Europe met to divide up the spoils of the war, had commenced on 23rd January 1919. Each nation had come with its own agenda: the Italians to dismember the Austro-Hungarian Empire; the French to disarm the Germans, regain Alsace and Lorraine and the Saar region and gain their share of the Ottoman Empire (including Syria); the British to win the German colonies in Africa and the South Pacific, keep control of Mesopotamia, have protectorates in Persia and Egypt and see the end of German naval power; and the Americans to establish their dream of a League of Nations. In addition, each one wanted control over oil.

Voyage to Bombay and Basra – October 1919

My last week in England was spent buying some suitable clothes for the tropics, packing, and saying farewell to everyone at Wenham. On Friday 26th September I caught an early train to Liverpool Street, and, as a railway strike was due to start at midnight, I took the train to Southampton that same afternoon, getting a room at the Dolphin Hotel for the night. I had instructions to board the troopship RIMS Dufferin at Southampton on Saturday 27th, but because of the rail strike the ship's departure was delayed and the Embarkation Officer said that it was unlikely to sail for two or three days.

With a couple of days to occupy unexpectedly, that afternoon I hired a bicycle and cycled to Cadnam Corner, Ringwood, and on to Wimborne, where I put up for the night at the Station Hotel. On Sunday morning I cycled to Dorchester and stayed with my old school friend Cyril, who was now a doctor, and Mrs Day. In Dorchester I caught up with Cyril's news, visited Mr Vidler at the Foundry, and called at the Barracks, before returning on Monday by boxcar to Tolpuddle, then by charabanc to Bournemouth and taxi to Southampton.

We boarded the Dufferin on the afternoon of the 30th and left Southampton dock at 9.00 am the following morning. Although the ship was bound for Bombay, instead of sailing westwards down the Channel, we headed back to Dungeness, where we picked up a pilot to take us to Gravesend and the East India Dock, in order to pick up 200 more passengers who had been stranded by the strike. The ship, already full, was now uncomfortably crowded with military personnel and some Government officials going to India. A few men had their wives on board; there were several ladies who were rejoining their husbands, having spent the summer in England, and two or three young ladies going out to marry.

I had a small cabin with three other army Majors on the lower deck; fortunately, it was an outside cabin with a porthole which, when the sea was calm, did not have to be closed. This was a troopship and not a luxury liner, and the

R.I.M.S. Dufferin

sailors and stewards all appeared to be natives, wearing turbans or scarlet fezes. Many were Mohammedans, who celebrated their 3-day Moharram festival with dancing and singing, mingling their religious music with Harry Lauder songs – the sublime and the ridiculous! Luckily the weather was kind, although there was a swell and the ship often rolled, but I survived without any serious seasickness.

The slow voyage to Bombay gave me an opportunity of making several new friends. One of them, Sir John Marshall, who was the Director-General of Archaeology in India, was especially interesting. He had been appointed by Lord Curzon in 1902 at the young age of 28 in order to take charge of the excavation, preservation, and repair of the multitude of ancient sites in that country. Educated at Cambridge, Marshall was noted for his courtesy, friendship, and hospitality, as well as for his brilliant conversation and tireless enthusiasm for the promotion of Indian archaeology.

We had many long talks covering topics of the day, including spiritualism. As the world emerged from the losses of the First World War and the influenza pandemic, so mediums and the psychical world had become big business, with associations and seances for people hoping to contact those they had lost. During one of our conversations he told me that he had been mystified, not being a spiritualist himself, by a seance which he had attended with the young daughter of a friend of his, who had developed the powers of a 'medium'. At his suggestion, she got in touch with the late Lord Byron (who died in 1824), because he, Sir John, knew much about his life and his haunts in Greece. Through this girl, who took down all her communications in writing, Lord Byron apparently gave several facts about his present 'life after death'. To check whether she was really communicating with the poet, Sir John asked for some proof of his identity. Immediately the girl started to take down, slowly and laboriously, a poem entitled 'Ode to a Moth Burnt in the Flame of a Candle', which she could not have composed on the spur of the moment. It was in Byron's style!

Lady Marshall, to whom he introduced me, was a charming, petite woman, very sensible and devoted to their 11-year-old daughter who was travelling with them. They knew and liked my recent boss, Colonel Battye, and his family in India, and we swapped some interesting stories. I occasionally played the piano in the saloon after dinner; sometimes playing a duet with Lady Marshall, or accompanying her and two other ladies who sang songs.

One of the officers in my cabin was Major Broad of the 5th Gurkhas; 'a very nice fellow, keen and capable; he expects to be going back to a good deal of scrapping on the NW Frontier during the winter'. At table I sat with the Garforth family and Mrs Lock, who was on her way back to her husband in Basra. I knew Major Garforth well when he and I were on the staff of Col. Battye in France. I also enjoyed conversations with others, including Mr Crapper, representing Manchester Cotton interests, Mr Keeling, Chief Engineer for New Delhi, and Mr King, Deputy Commissioner of Lahore.

We reached Port Said, after 10 days at sea, on 12th October - it was extremely hot. I went ashore with Major Chadwick and some of the ladies, and we had dinner at the Eastern Exchange Hotel. It was the first time I had set foot on African soil. After dinner we went to the Simon Arzt store, which had stayed open especially for us, and I bought a topee and some light clothing. Simon Arzt was a New York Jew, who had gone to Port Said as a merchant and manufacturer of Turkish tobacco in 1869, and established a store which was to become famous as the main department store in town. The next morning we took several ladies ashore, and breakfasted on the cool verandah of the Casino Palace Hotel, out of the blazing sunshine, before going to the shops - ladies were not allowed to go unescorted.

The ship spent the day coaling and re-provisioning in Port Said and was covered in a fine coal dust when we returned; it had to be hosed down before we left port and entered the Suez Canal. There we saw the war bridge across the canal, and the Palestine army camp at Kantara, where 14,000 troops were still stationed. It was getting much hotter, and many of those who did not have an outside cabin went onto the deck to sleep until 5.30 am, when the reveille bugle woke them, and daily scrubbing of the decks took place. On the deck at night, the port side was for men only, the aft part for ladies only, and the starboard side was for husbands with wives. There was little space between the narrow single mattresses which had to be placed rather close together, husbands sometimes waking up close to another man's wife!

Between 6.00 and 7.00 am most of us met in the saloon for 'chota hazri', an early breakfast of tea, bread and butter and marmalade; the women dressed in slippers and dressing gowns and the men in pyjamas or bath gowns. The maximum speed allowed through the Canal was 7 miles per hour, and so it took us 13 hours to cover the 90-100 miles to Suez. By the time we entered the Red Sea the heat was appalling - I had never experienced such heat and humidity before - cabin temperatures were up to 96 degrees (all temperatures were measured in Fahrenheit). Although we had two ceiling fans in our cabin, I joined those sleeping on deck. The days were spent in shirt sleeves and shorts, but a tunic had to be worn in the dining saloon and occasionally black tie for a special evening. In the Red Sea we had the misfortune of a following wind, and so for a while we felt no air movement at all. After it died down, the ship's movement created a welcome breeze, and we eventually encountered a dry head wind, which made conditions much more comfortable.

Almost 5 days after leaving Port Said we reached Aden and went ashore to visit the Tanks, ancient reservoirs created out of rocky basins thousands of years ago. Unfortunately, they had been reconstructed with large quantities of masonry in 1899 and little of their ancient origin was visible. Aden, an English colony, a garrison town, and a coaling station, was a dry, rocky, desolate place where drinking and washing water was rationed, as it all had to be distilled from seawater. We returned to the ship at 6.15 pm, shortly before the dressing bell went for dinner.

From Aden, it was another five days before we reached Bombay - the 2½ week voyage was one of the most tedious I have experienced, although it did give me the opportunity of reading up on Mesopotamia before I arrived there. I noted in my diary that 'some of the women on board do require a lot of attention! Mrs Garforth Senior (probably 63) requires her long lounge chair to be moved several times a day, in order to find the exact position where the sun is not too hot, the glare from the sea not too bright, the breeze not too little or too much, and the smell or heat from the downstairs ventilators not too pronounced! I often detach myself from other passengers and sit on a camp stool, either reading or writing letters'.

We docked in Bombay on the morning of October 24th, and I was able to do some sight-seeing for a few days whilst waiting for the next ship to take me to Basra. I stayed in the luxurious flat of a bachelor friend, E. Robert H. Jackson, in Evelyn House, Apollo Bunda. He had six Indian servants: 2 bearers, 1 cook and an assistant, a motor car boy, and a coolie; their efficiency impressed me greatly, and I learned that they were only paid a total of about 120 rupees per month (say £2 in 2010 money).

Bombay was hot and humid, and the temperature rose from 79 degrees minimum at night to 90 degrees at midday. Events, scenes, and sensations passed with kaleidoscopic rapidity. I did some shopping, visited the zoo and the botanical gardens, and entertained the Garforths and Mrs Lock to dinner at the Taj Mahal Hotel.

One day I was invited by Sir John Marshall to accompany him, his daughter Margaret, and her governess, together with his Babu secretary, on an official inspection of the ancient Buddhist rock-hewn caves or temples on Elephanta Island. We went across the bay in the smart official launch of the Governor of Bombay. It was my first experience of tropical jungle, and, as the track up to one of the caves was steep, Sir John was carried in a chair.

Sir John Marshall, his 11-year-old daughter Margaret and her governess on a Government launch going to see the caves on Elephanta Island (above)

Sir John Marshall being carried in a chair by Indian bearers on Elephanta Island (right)

Arrival in Mesopotamia

I left Bombay on 28th October on the RIMS Northbrook, a sister ship of the Dufferin. We stopped at Karachi to embark 500 native troops and eventually reached Basra, a busy port with miles of wharves at the head of the Persian Gulf, on 5th November, thirty-six days after leaving Southampton. The last 90 miles was up the Shatt-al-Arab waterway, the name given to the combined Tigris and Euphrates after their junction. Today, troopships would take a fraction of the time, and I would have been sent by air.

From the Northbrook, I transferred to a small steamer, and was taken to the naval dockyard at Ma-aqil (hereafter spelt Maqil), and from there by lorry to the British Base at Makina, where I spent the night in a tent with Major Priaulx Groves. I acquired an Indian 'bearer' and, after a couple of days in camp, Lt.Col. Samuel Smith arranged a room for me at the River Front Hotel in Basra, run by the Government to accommodate senior officers and their families passing through.

On the waterfront stood those old Basra houses made of yellow baked bricks, their lattice wooden balconies leaning out over the streets crowded with Arabs. After only a few days in the hotel, I was awakened in the middle of the night by a lot of noise and the glare of fire. The hotel was in flames and my new Indian bearer, with singular coolness and pluck, helped in saving my kit, much of which was thrown to the ground from the upstairs balcony outside my room. On the following day, I left on board a Tigris river steamer for Baghdad with Pte. E. Bennett and my Indian bearer, arriving at Hinaidi five days later.

The three things which I noticed most during those first few days in Mesopotamia were:

- the soft, almost white dust, like talcum powder, which covered everything;
- the size of Basra and the British military base there, covering 20 square miles; and
- my distinctly unfavourable impression of the local Arabs.

Mesopotamia

Mesopotamia - the land 'between the rivers' - was the historical region centred on the Tigris and Euphrates river systems, roughly corresponding today to Iraq and Kuwait, and including parts of northern Saudi Arabia, eastern Syria, south-eastern Turkey and Kurdistan. Both rivers had their source in the Taurus Mountains and were liable to overflow when the snows in the mountains melted, sometimes causing great catastrophic floods like the Flood in the book of Genesis. On the Tigris the annual flood reached its height in May and on the Euphrates a month later. But in recent years flood escapes have been designed to divert excess water into the lower desert areas, thus protecting Baghdad and other towns from serious inundation.

Journey up the Tigris to Bagdad

The Tigris river steamer was being used as a hospital ship. As the senior officer on board, I was OC, and therefore entitled to the only passenger cabin available, in which I spread myself comfortably. There were a few other British officers on board, as well as 103 Ghurkhas.

Hospital ship No. I, bearing sick and wounded from Kut, coming alongside the bank of the Tigris at the British lines at Falahiyah.

The Tigris river steamer, a stern-wheeler, being used as a hospital ship

After leaving Maqil we passed Kurnah and Ozier (or Ezra's Tomb) where we entered the Narrows, a 28 mile stretch of water from Ozier to Qalat Saleh. Whilst we were tied up, Capt. C.H. Kindersley and I went for a walk across country with shot guns after partridge, but with no luck. After Amara the country became devoid of trees or serious cultivation; there were a few palm groves and Arab encampments of open tents or rush-work shelters, some sheep, a few cattle and horses, and dozens of camels. We did not get any more shooting, but saw some jackals, many flocks of sand-grouse, and a few pelicans and ducks.

We arrived at Kut on 18th November, too late for the train to Baghdad, and so stayed on board for the night. The next morning I visited Lt. Davidson RE of the Electrical and Mechanical (E&M) Section at the Depot, and he showed me over the power plant, the ice plants (4 tons/day and 1 ton/day), and the filtration and chlorination plant (2 x 6,000 gals/hr). In the afternoon I went with Capt. Kindersley and Lt. Trask into Kut to see the British cemetery and the bazaar, before we boarded the train for the journey across 100 miles of desert to Baghdad, arriving at Hinaidi station at 6.45 am on 20th November.

My first few days in Baghdad were taken up settling in, meeting my staff, and making familiarisation visits to the Hinaidi filtration plant, a flour mill, a meat freezing plant, our dairy farms, the workshops, a new jetty, and the site of a new pumping station. Having seen what was available in the town, I wrote to Selfridges with a cheque for £3 and ordered 4 lbs biscuits, 1 lb tea, 4 tins shoe polish, 2 toothpaste, 1 box soap, 1 Brouer (a type of bookcase and cabinet), 300 loose leaves, and 125 envelopes which I could not find locally.

Baghdad

Baghdad is an ancient city with its own mystique; it was here in the tenth century AD that Scheherazade told of golden palaces and silver ponds, eunuchs and slaves, Ali Baba, and Aladdin. The citadel on the Tigris was founded as the capital of the Islamic empire by the Abbasid caliph Al-Mansur in 762 A.D, a century after the death of the prophet Muhammad. The heart of the Abbasid Caliphate, it flourished for 500 years as one of the largest, most prosperous cities in the world with more than a million people of many races and creeds.

The Baghdad of a thousand years ago was sophisticated and cosmopolitan, its writers produced some of the greatest Arab literature, translated Plato and Aristotle into Arabic; its mathematicians, using Arabic numbers, introduced the concept of zero; its scientists built an astronomical observatory and studied the round surface of the earth. Arab traders dealt in gold from Africa, silver from India, porcelain from China and pearls from the Gulf.

But history swept much of that away. The tyrannical force of the Mongols, the feudal rule of the Persians, the corrupt occupation of the Turks, together with plagues and floods, had wiped out most of the city. When the British troops arrived in 1917 it consisted of only two thousand people living in shabby buildings inside crumbling city walls. Yet a few grand Ottoman buildings survived, and slender minarets and domed mosques glittered in the sun. Statuesque palm groves and verdant gardens brought relief from the dry hot sun.

It did not take long for the British, under General Maude, newly appointed Military Commander of Mesopotamia, to spiffy up the place with horse races, polo matches, cribbage and dominoes, afternoon tea and lawn tennis.

My Contract

It was not until 1st February 1920, after I had met with Major General E.H. de Vere Atkinson, Chief Engineer, that I was formally demobilized from Military Service and became a British Gazetted Official with the status of Lieutenant Colonel, on a standard one year contract with the E&M Directorate of Mesopotamia at a salary of 1600/- Rupees/month. The contract was technically with the 'Government of Mesopotamia' and provided first class passages to and from my home to Basra, with full pay during furlough, which in my case was 60 days per year. Accommodation was provided free of charge, together with rations and medical and hospital attendance in Army facilities.

Appointment as Assistant Director of Works Mesopotamian Expeditionary Force

My appointment to the position of Assistant Director of Works and Director of the Electrical and Mechanical (E&M) Services of the Mesopotamian Expeditionary Force, the British Army of Occupation, took effect from 28th January 1920, when I took over from Lt.Col. Maclean, who was being demobilized and returning to England. I inherited his big German Nusseldorfer car, together with his driver and his batman, but I retained my own Indian bearer.

It was my job to provide the essential supplies of drinking water, electricity, and even ice, for all the British forces stationed in thirteen garrisons or cantonments in Mespot, as it was popularly called, and to four more garrisons temporarily in NW Persia. As well as supplying services to the three most important garrisons in the cities of Baghdad, Basra (in the south) and Mosul (in the north), I had to supply troops to run installations in the settlements of Hillah (Babylon), Dewaniyeh, Ramadi and Hit on the Euphrates; Shergat, Baiji, Tekrit, Amara and Kut on the Tigris; Baqubah and Kirkuk in Kurdistan, and also Karind, Kermanshah, Hamadan, and Kasvin in Persia, where I had a search-light section.

When I wrote to my parents in February, I included the following list of officers on my staff with their responsibilities:

- Capt. D.B. Webbe — Personal Assistant - Baghdad HQ Office
- Maj. F.V. Jordan RE — Mosul (Northern Area) power stations, ice plants & pumping stations   -
- Lt. White — Qaiyarah oil wells and refinery
- Capt. Forbes — Water supplies (about 40 pumping stations driven by oil engines, 24 filtration plants and irrigation barges)
- Maj. Low — Electrical installations in new cantonments with 3 officers and 250 men
- Lt. Venour Duncan — Personnel Administrator of about 2,000 enlisted men
- Supt. Cunningham — Electrical power stations in Baghdad local area (about 10 different plants including the central power station)
- Lt. Gateley — Electrical Assistant for out-station extensions
- Capt. Tudsbery RE — Design and the drawing office
- Capt. Midgeley RE — Baghdad Water Supply Extension Scheme

Officers in charge of out-stations:

Kermanshah & Persian lines of communication	- Lt. H.W. Lane
Baiji, Tekrit, Qaiyarah, Samarra (under Mosul)	- Major Jordan
Hillah, Dewaniyeh and Kufa (on the Euphrates)	- Lt. Edmunds
Kut and Amara (on the Tigris)	- Lt. Bertram
Shergat	- Lt. Finlayson

APPOINTMENTS, PROMOTIONS, REWARDS, Etc.

Approved by the General Officer Commanding-in-Chief, Mesopotamian Expeditionary Force.

List No. 4.

GENERAL HEAD QUARTERS,
MESOPOTAMIAN EXPEDITIONARY FORCE,
28th January, 1920.

COMMANDS AND STAFF.

The undermentioned appointments are made :—

1. **General Officer Commanding-in-Chief (acting).**
   Mes. Ex. Force—Maj.-Genl. G. A. J. Leslie, C.B., C.M.G., G.O.C., 17th (Indian) Div. *vice* Maj.-Genl. Sir G. F. MacMunn, K.C.B., K.C.S.I., D.S.O., (to India)—dated 24th Jan., 1920.
   [Authy. :—W.O. telegram No. 35100, M.S.I.A., dated 10th Jan., 1920].

2. **Commander, Royal Artillery.**
   18th (Indian) Div.—Bt. Col. (temp. Brig.-Genl.) W. P. L. Davies, C.M.G., D.S.O., R.A., from B.G.R.A., G H.Q., *vice* Lt.-Col. (temp. Brig.-Genl.) F. A. Buzzard, D.S.O., R.A. (to home establishment)—dated 5th Jan., 1920.

3. **Brigade Major, Royal Artillery.**
   18th (Indian) Div.—Temp. Lt. (temp. Capt.) R. H. Cameron, R.A., from S.C., R.A., *vice* Capt. H. F. C. Kempe, M.C., R.A. (to home establishment)—dated 25th Dec., 1919.

4. **Deputy Director of Labour (Cl 'T').**
   Bt. Maj. (temp. Brig.-Genl.) F. D. Frost, C.B.E., M.C., S. & T. Corps, from Director of Labour (Cl. 'S') and reverts to temp. Col. whilst so employed—dated 26th Jan., 1920.

5. **Assistant Director of Veterinary Services.**
   Bt. Col. F. W. Hunt, C.M.G., C.B.E., R.A.V.C., *vice* Bt. Lt.-Col. P. J. Harris, R.A.V.C. (to S.V.O., Base)—dated 14th Jan., 1920.

6. **Assistant Director of Works (Cl, 'X').**
   Temp. Maj. H C Lott, M.C., R.E., and to be temp. Lt.-Col. whilst so employed, *vice* Temp. Lt. (temp. Lt.-Col.) A. McLean, R E., (to U.K. for demobilization)—dated 1st Jan., 1920.

7. **Assistant Director of Ordnance Services.**
   G.H.Q.—Maj & O.O. 3rd Class (temp. Lt.-Col & O O 2nd class) K. L. Stevenson, R.A.O.C., and to be actg. Lt.-Col. whilst so employed, *vice* Temp. Capt. (actg. Lt.-Col.) C. H. Mapleson, R.A.O.C. (to D.A.D O S., G.H.Q.)—dated 23rd Dec., 1919.
   [Authy. :—W.O. letter No. 100/A.O.D./621 (M.S.-4-E.) dated 11th Aug., 1919].

8. **Deputy Assistant Director of Ordnance Services.**
   G.H.Q.—Temp. Capt. (actg. Lt.-Col.) C. H. Mapleson, R.A.O.C., from A.D.O.S, G.H.Q, and reverts to actg. Maj. whilst so employed, to complete establishment—dated 23rd Dec., 1919.
   [Authy. :—W.O. telegram No. 100/A.O.D./621 (M.S.-4. E.) dated 11th Aug., 1919].

The Work House – our billet and mess in Baghdad

15

A sketch of The Work House by one of our officers

We called our Senior Works Directorate mess in Baghdad 'The Work House'; it was one of several GHQ messes and consisted mostly of Lieutenant Colonels, with a couple of Majors, and two Lieutenants RE. One of the latter was John Glubb who later became famous, first as Glubb Pasha, leader of the Arab Legion, and eventually as Lt.Gen. Sir John Bagot Glubb.

GLUBB PASHA
Leads his "Girls"

My batman and Indian bearer   Lt. John Glubb

In 1971 Glubb published an analysis of the struggle between the Arabs and the Jews, in a book entitled 'Peace in the Holy Land'. In Trevor Royle's biography of 'Glubb Pasha', he describes him as a man of his time and class, inspired by the high-minded notions of empire, but equally loyal to his Arab friends, and whose passionate empathy with Arabic aspirations and culture endowed him with glamour and legend.

Another equally lively young officer was Lt. Laurence Douglas Grand, who eventually became Major General Grand, Director of Works and Buildings at the War Office. With young Glubb and Grand, and also Lt.Col. Mousley DSO RE, I enjoyed several weekend shooting trips in the desert.

My Team of Officers and Men

The area I had to cover was about 800 miles east to west and 300 miles north to south. Besides having a team of Army officers, all of them engineers, under my command and administration, I also had about 8,000 men most of whom were civilians. The majority of these were locally recruited Arabs and Persians, with a few Baghdadi Jews, and even a few Chinese.

For skilled craftsmen such as electricians, mechanics, and wiremen, also clerks and store-keepers, I had several companies of enrolled Indians from the Indian Army, including Hindus and Muslims, Sikhs, and Punjabis; this was long before Partition in 1947. The Indians were highly skilled and were indispensable in running the electric power stations, erecting power lines, wiring barracks and working as brick-makers, patternmakers, etc. Each company had its own British officers and NCO's, and Sikhs predominated amongst the mechanics and electricians.

My Personal Assistant, Capt. D.B. Webbe, an Anglo-Indian from the Indian Army, was wonderfully good in relieving me of an immense amount of correspondence. He drafted most of the replies to letters and applications, and had them typed, before giving me them to sign. When a letter was obviously more important, he attached a note to the file with all the information on the subject, so that the whole history of the case was immediately in front of me before I replied. However, not long after my arrival I received letters from some of the more restive Indians, complaining about minor grievances, such as the food they were served and the way in which it was prepared, which did not conform to their dietary preferences and Brahmin principles.

Dated 26.1.1920.

To
The Assistant Director of Works,
(E. & M.) R.E., Baghdad.

Sir,

We the two undermentioned servants of your department, having been undergoing penitable and handsome difficulties regarding our food arrangements and being becoming
weaker and weaker day by day in health, humbly, faithfully,
and in an obedient manner, beg to request that you will be
kind enough to wipe out our troubles and grant us a fresh
life after considering our grievances stated below :-

1. The cook who prepares and serves us our food is a
strict non vegetarian who is accustomed to kill and eat
fowls etc. Because his hands contain the blood of those
poor birds when killed in our presence, we are neither able
to see his hands or eat food which he prepares and gives as
there is smell of above in it frequently and as he does
such deeds which are against our Brahmin principles and
habits of the community.

In short the manner of food which is prepared by
him, is not at all suitable for our health or for our satis-
faction. As there are no strict Vegitanian cooks available in our section we humbly request you to kindly grant
us ration and servant allowance, permitting us to get our
food cooked under our instructions and shifting us to a
separate place where the killing etc. are not to be done in
our presence. Otherwise we who already underwent suffer-
ings of stomach derangements are afraid that we get our
health spoiled still the more and have to undergo medical
treatments, thereby causing loss to Govt: works and money.

Thanking you in anticipation and hoping to be
favoured with the ration allowance etc. requested above,

We thankfully beg to remain, Sir,

Your most obedient servants,

WD.139.5 Braj Lal.   General Clerk
                                    (Telephone).

.... WD.17873 E. & M. Store.

Letter of complaint from an Indian soon after my arrival in Baghdad.

They had been unable to get any response from Webbe, who had
demonstrated his efficiency and authority by dismissing their
complaints out of hand. Feeling that they had not received fair
treatment, they took the opportunity of appealing to the higher

authority of their new master. I made it known that I was accessible to any of the men at any time when they knocked on the glass door of my office. Almost immediately the complaints ceased, or were much more humanely dealt with by my PA. This was one of my earlier successes in handling the hundreds of Indians working in my departments in Baghdad, and helped to establish my reputation for fairness.

I was also fortunate in my immediate chief, the Director of E&M Works, Lt.Col. Bridcut, with whom I got on well. He was a highly active and far-seeing man, two or three years younger than me (I was then 37); he was extremely capable and even-tempered.

Our Work

Our work in the E&M Section involved looking after the existing electricity generating and water supply facilities, as well as constructing new installations to service the British garrisons (cantonments), and in some cases the local population, throughout Mesopotamia and parts of Persia. During 1920 we were installing new electrical power plants at:

- Karind, consisting of two 40 hp diesel coupled oil engine dynamo sets for the large married family camp for the summer;
- Kermanshah, consisting of an additional 24 hp Hornsby engine;
- Kirkuk, consisting of two 26 hp Blackstone oil engines with belt driven dynamos;
- Tekrit, consisting of a 36 hp Ruston engine with belt drive; and
- Dewanyeh, consisting of two 10 kW diesel coupled steam sets.

We were also installing new pumping stations and building hospitals, as well as managing the workshops, and undertaking any repair and maintenance work required.

Some of the water-supply plants which we had to manage were elaborately equipped floating pumping stations on barges on the Tigris, each having on its operating staff an analytical chemist. In order to save the cost of heavy masonry pump pits, I fitted up some unwanted 150ft long steel barges with 55 hp oil engines driving 12-inch centrifugal pumps for irrigating British Army farms. The main function of the farms was to grow lucerne (alfalfa), which could be cut up to twelve times a year, as feedstock for Army animals. The Tigris river level varied over 20 ft during the year, and the heavy erosive action of the river in flood was liable to scour away any installation within 2 or 3 years. Each flood season a few Arab irrigation stations fell into the river and I was expecting an electric sub-station building to be washed away by a flood in April, even though the riverbank was presently 60ft away.

We had three 150-ton refrigeration barges (with Pelapone engines) on the Tigris, in which my 'refrigeration officer' received and stored 1,000 tons of frozen meat from Army bases in Malta and Britain. The meat, sometimes stored for periods up to five years, was more palatable than locally killed stock.

Inspection Visits

During the next three weeks I spent most of the time in my office and the workshops, and getting to know my colleagues in the Army establishment in Baghdad. I also had to prepare a budget and estimate of expenses for the E&M Section for 1920-21.

At my first guest night in our mess in December we entertained Brig.Gen. Percy Hambro DQMG, Lt.Col. R.C. Wilson, Major Griffith (Finance), Lt.Col. Boyd (OC Royal Air Force in Mesopotamia – 2 squadrons), Lt.Col. Lane (I.M.S) and Major Chrystal (3rd Hussars). After dinner we played bridge and vingt-et-un until midnight and eventually turned in about 1.00 am. A week later, after another dinner with Lt.Col. Bridcut and Major

General Atkinson, followed by vingt-et-un, I received my contract from the General confirming my position and pay of 1,600 Rupees per month, which seemed perfectly acceptable.

I then set about arranging visits to inspect each of the facilities for which I was responsible. On my first visit, I went with my bearer and an Arab driver 70 miles west of Baghdad to Ramadi, in our Model T Ford, equipped with spare tyres and lamps, as well as blankets and provisions, a primus stove, and bottles of water, in case of a breakdown in the desert. Darkness fell as we passed Fallujah and, although I had been told that the road across the desert was straightforward, I had to get out at times in order to find the tracks in the darkness, as our feeble lamps did not provide sufficient light.

My Ford car - 1920

In Ramadi I put up as a guest of Major Kenist of the 10th Indian Lancers and dined in his comfortable mess, a former hospital, warmed by a fire which was burning lumps of bitumen from Hit, 30 miles upstream on the Euphrates. As the next day was Sunday, I decided to visit Hit to see and photograph the hot spring which was continually bringing up a scum of bitumen or pitch. The bitumen was being skimmed off by the Arabs who used it for caulking or sealing their locally made boats, just as God instructed Noah to 'pitch the Ark within and without with pitch'.

The Greek traveller Herodotus described these bitumen springs (at a place he called Is) when he passed through the Babylon area 450 years before Christ. Hit is not far from the place where the Tower of Babel and other similar Ziggurats were built and its pitch was almost certainly the 'slime' mentioned in the book of Genesis, when it was decided to build the Tower of Babel using bricks and 'slime' for mortar.

W. H. Allen, Sons and Co Ltd

10-KW STEAM GENERATING SET—ALLEN

10 kW Steam Generating Set

A spring of bitumen or pitch at Hit

At Ramadi I had a detachment of 45 men running an electric light plant, a 1½ ton/day ice plant, and a pumping plant with an elaborate filtration plant which I planned to move to Baghdad. One engine and pump was supplying water to a farm growing fodder for a cavalry regiment. The station was being run by an English NCO and, before I left, I told him that I had decided to reduce his staff by 10 men. Amongst his staff were 9 cooks employed to satisfy the dietary requirements of at least six religions or castes amongst the gang!

On another visit, I went in the Ford to Hillah with an Indian electrical subordinate, to inspect our out-station there run by Lt. Edmonds. We had had some tyre trouble on the way and, after being shown round the power house and the pumping and filtration plant, we called upon Major and Mrs King Mason about a spare car for the following day. They gave us an excellent dinner in the mess, and I shared the Major's bedroom for the night. The next morning we set off in the two cars for Dewaniyeh, where I investigated a proposal which had been sanctioned, to put in an electric lighting installation of two steam 10 kW generating sets with a street distribution system costing altogether Rps.52,000, or £5,500 in money of the day.

We stayed the night at a very hospitable mess commanded by Major Stewart and had a delicious dinner of wild duck and trifle. The next morning we set off for home on a shocking road, or more accurately a track, and finished up with a broken car with a broken spring in the open desert, 15 miles from Baghdad, just as darkness was falling. Fortunately, I was given a lift in another old Ford, passing most opportunely, and reached Baghdad that night. My Indian subordinate, dressed as well as any West London 'swell', and the Arab driver spent the night with our car, and I sent a lorry at day-break to bring them and the broken car back to our workshops.

Visit to Persia for Christmas 1919
Alfred and Maude Tayler & Doris (Lessing)

Just before Christmas 1919 I set off by train from Baghdad with Lt.Col. Bridcut, and with our big 'Juggernaut' as we called the Nusseldorfer, loaded onto a wagon. The train took us 130 miles out of Baghdad to Quraitu, the railhead for our troops in Persia, in the foothills of the Push-ti-ku Mountains, close to the Persian frontier. There we disembarked and unloaded our car and bulky luggage. There were four of us, as we had brought a bearer and a motor mechanic, and we each had sleeping kit for the frosty weather in the mountains.

My German Nusseldorfer

The car managed to climb the Paitak pass without difficulty and that evening we reached Karind, above the snow line, about 4,500 ft above Baghdad. There we were given a room by our hosts, the Sappers & Miners Company, in a house with a roof but no doors or windows!

On Christmas morning more snow threatened, so we set off early to pick up Col. Gaskell DSO CRE at Hassanabad camp.

Thereafter our troubles began with a puncture and then, at the foot of the pass, we had ignition trouble, and spent 3½ hours taking the magneto apart to try to get a 'fat' spark. Finally Col. Gaskell's own car came to the rescue and we reached Kermanshah in time to change for Christmas dinner. Col. Bridcut stayed at Col. Gaskell's mess whilst I was a guest of Mr Cave, the local director of the Imperial Bank of Persia, and Alfred and Maude Tayler at The Bank House, by far the most luxuriously furnished house in town.

The Bank House in Kermanshah where Doris Lessing was born

At the Bank House, Kermanshah

Our dinner at the Bank House was magnificent - the cooking, the table linen, the silver, and glass, all being of the very best. In addition to Col. Bridcut, Col. Gaskell and me, the company included two ladies en route with the husband of one of them to Tehran, a padre, an American missionary and two young doctors, altogether a dozen of us. Afterwards we played parlour games, such as 'Up Jenkins' and other frivolous amusements, until 2.30 am when everyone dispersed.

Alfred Tayler was a cousin and old friend of mine from East Anglia, who had been given a job in a bank after the War. As a Captain during the War he had been badly wounded; he had had one leg amputated and suffered terribly from shell shock. He vividly recalled and spoke passionately of the soldiers who, shell-shocked like himself, or unable to get themselves out of their mud holes to face the enemy, might be shot for cowardice. "It could have been me", he used to say, "It was just luck that it wasn't."

Alfred married Emily Maude McVeigh, an Irish girl who had nursed him back to health in the Royal Free Hospital in London. As soon as he was fit enough he felt that he had to leave England; he never forgave his country for what he saw as promises betrayed. After they married, he persuaded his bank to send him to the Imperial Bank of Persia in Kermanshah, where their two children were born, Doris on 22nd October 1919, and Harry in December 1921. Harry was named after me and I was to be his godfather. Doris later became well-known internationally as the writer Doris Lessing; she was made a Companion of Honour in 1999 and awarded the Nobel Prize for Literature in 2007.

Doris wrote an interesting, two-part biography of her parents entitled 'Alfred and Emily', describing their rather unhappy life together in Rhodesia, where they went after Persia, and how they might have been if things had worked out differently. In her autobiography, 'Under my Skin', Doris mentioned that I had come to visit her parents when they were living in Persia and she was still a baby. She wrote, 'It is strange that of this man (Harry Lott) who my father talked of so often, for so many years, I can say nothing, for I don't remember him. Uncle Harry Lott was the family's good friend. He sent presents and wrote letters, and that went on when we were in Africa too. Oh, he did love you kids: "he couldn't get enough of you," said Daddy, adding characteristically, "God knows why".' She added 'And now I watch some little child in the arms of a loving friend and know that this will affect the child for always, like a little secret store of goodness, or one of those pills with a delayed reaction.'

On Boxing Day morning, I went to inspect 'my' power station and workshop in Kermanshah with a guide provided by Mr Cave who sent one of his security guards with me. Like most of the local towns, there were no streets wide enough for two motor cars to pass, and I eventually reached my destination through narrow, muddy lanes about 7ft wide. I spent a busy morning with the NCO in charge and returned the next day to inspect the books with the storekeeper. After tiffin at 1.30 pm at Col. Gaskell's, four of us went shooting in the afternoon, walking along streams and beside vineyards looking for game. Our bag at the end of the day comprised only 3 woodcock and one snipe, all shot by Capt. Moore.

The next day Mr Cave had a distinguished visitor, Emir Nizam, a Persian prince of great wealth, who had been partly educated in England and appointed Governor of the Province of Kermanshah. Whisky and cigarettes were passed around, and his companion talked in French (not knowing English) to Mrs Tayler.

On Sunday we took a picnic to Tak-i-Bustan, in the heart of the Zagros Mountains, about 10 miles away, to see one of Persia's ancient relics of the Sassanid dynasty. All six of us, Col. Bridcut, Mr Cave, Mr and Mrs Tayler, Capt. Moore, and me, piled into our car and the Indian motor mechanic sat on a tin of petrol on the footboard outside. We set off at noon, but were delayed for half an hour by a puncture, before reaching the foot of the mountain which rose almost perpendicularly out of the plain.

Our picnic party in the Nusseldorfer

Picnic with Alfred & Maude Tayler at Tak-i-Bustan on Boxing Day 1919

The remarkable 4th century rock carvings in the cliff face showed scenes of the investiture of Shapur III (383-388), and one depicted Darius, another great Persian king. On two walls there were hunting scenes with horses, deer, and pig-sticking events, processions of laden camels and donkeys, and a deer hunt on horseback. We unpacked our luncheon baskets and ate partridge pie, tarts, cakes, and cheese, and had beer, followed by coffee from a Thermos flask.

The next morning we left Kermanshah and headed back to Baghdad. I had not been long in Mesopotamia and was very conscious of not wanting to be seen to go 'joy-riding' to Tehran, although it was not far beyond the end of the road at Kasvin. Nor did I visit the men of my search-light section at Enzeli, a port and popular seaside resort on the Caspian Sea.

On the way back we soon encountered tyre trouble and it took us 4 hours to cover the first 10 miles, after which the magneto played up again and we wondered if we would have to spend a cold night on the roadside in the mountains. Our journey took us over a series of passes, across mountain ridges, between which were wide fertile plains and a few partly destroyed villages. The villages had suffered when the Russian army retreated before the Turks, having just failed to join up with the British forces in Mesopotamia. We saw that villagers were returning gradually and building themselves shelters of reeds and boughs. Eventually we arrived by nightfall at Karind, where we enjoyed the hospitality of the Sapper & Miners Company who put us up once again in their mess.

Baghdad 1920

Within an hour of leaving Karind the next morning, our car came off worse in an encounter with a large boulder, and we had to abandon it on the roadside, and beg lifts for ourselves and our luggage, from passing Ford cars which were already loaded to capacity. Gradually we reached the railhead and arrived back in Baghdad on New Year's Eve.

I spent New Year's Day 1920 in the office going through arrears of correspondence. I also received half a dozen new officers, just out from England or France, all ignorant, like myself, of the local conditions and the Hindustani language. However, they would become useful, and I posted them to some of the E&M out-stations which we were managing.

During 1920, leaving Capt. Webbe in charge of my Baghdad office, I made many inspections of the various branches of my command, sometimes travelling by car, the Model T Ford or the German Nusseldorfer, or by Government launch on the Tigris, and often by train. Whenever possible, I visited the nearby Biblical sites, such as the Tree of Knowledge at Kurnah, 40 miles upstream from Amara.

 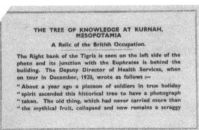

The Tree of Knowledge at Kurnah   Kurnah, 40 miles upstream from Amara.

Kurnah is where the Tigris and Euphrates join - it must have seemed like a garden to weary travellers from the desert, with its palm groves and pomegranate trees and a kind of willow growing along the riverbank. The whole place was green and surrounded by marsh and reed-beds. It matters not that Eve's tree is not an apple, or anything like it, as it serves its symbolic purpose in the area traditionally believed to be the Garden of Eden.

Travels in Mesopotamia were rarely without incident; metalled roads in the European sense hardly existed, and cars frequently broke down and had punctures, due to the rough surfaces and hot, dusty conditions. After a heavy storm, nowhere else in the world could movement become more difficult more quickly, or indeed impossible for a time, as the rain turned the argillaceous soil into a slippery, muddy mess.

In February I made a visit to Dewaniyeh, where we were installing an electrical system paid for by the local civilian population. I took the midnight train from Baghdad, and spent a couple of days with Lt. Edmonds inspecting the works there, and also at Hillah (near the ruins of Babylon) where we operated filtration presses, a flour mill, and ice works.

From Hillah we drove via Kufa to visit Najaf, the third holiest city of Shia Islam (the others being Mecca and Karbala). Najaf, the burial place of Muhammad's son-in-law and cousin, Ali ibn Ali Talib, was traditionally the starting point of the Hajj for Shiite pilgrims from Persia to Mecca. The only British there were the Political Officer, whose guest I was, his doctor, a police officer, the Assistant Political Officer (APO), and an office superintendent.

The mosque and shrine of Ali ibn Ali Talib in Najaf

32

In March 1919, the inhabitants of Najaf had become fanatical and rebellious and it had required two 6" guns to quell the rebellion. The British then destroyed a line of small shops, built just inside the walls of the city, to make a road wide enough for armoured cars, in the event of future trouble. When we visited everything was quiet, and we were being begged to install a water supply for its 40,000 inhabitants.

The walled city of Najaf as it was in 1920

The purpose of my visit was to make a preliminary reconnaissance for the scheme. It seemed that the water supply would have to come by a 6 mile long open channel from Abu Shukhair, on the main branch of the Euphrates, into settling ponds, and then be pumped to large 100,000 gallon tanks, 250 feet above the pumping stations, on existing mounds. I went with the APO to Abu Shukhair where, as we walked through the town, the whole Arab population stood up and saluted, a few of the leading Arabs shook our hands, and the Arab guard turned out and presented arms!

Later in the month I spent a week visiting Kingerbah and Kirkuk, staying with Lt. King in the 9th Sappers and Miners camp in Kingerbah, and with Lt. Gowens, who had come out on the Dufferin with me, in the Works billet in Kirkuk. The overnight train journey to Kingerbah was delayed by a few hours when our train collided with another at Quaraghan; it then took us another 5½ hours to drive the last 75 miles to Kirkuk, as the rail did not extend that far. In Kirkuk we were putting in a water supply and electrical installation, principally to power fans in the summer months for the garrison, which was based in an old Turkish fort just outside the town. I visited the site and attended a conference of the 52nd Brigade officers to discuss our services, and spent an afternoon visiting the famous oil springs and gas springs.

Kirkuk in Kurdistan

In the desert around Kirkuk, just inside Kurdistan, where years later the great producing wells of the Iraq Petroleum Company would yield over 1 million barrels of oil a month, there was a most extraordinary patch of ground, hardly a mile square, containing four remarkable natural phenomena. In one corner there was a cold-water spring, flowing into another spring of hot sulphurous water a little lower down.

Not far from this was an area where flames of burning natural gas, issuing from fissures in the rocks, were rising two foot or so from the ground; they were almost colourless in the daytime, but smelled strongly of sulphur and lit up the area at night.

The Eternal fires of Baba Gurgur at Kirkuk

These were the Eternal Fires of Baba Gurgur (meaning the 'Father of Fire') which had been burning for at least 2,300 years, and were seen by Alexander the Great. Although Daniel is supposed to be buried at Kirkuk, there is apparently no support for the story that the Eternal Fires were the 'burning fiery furnace' in the Book of Daniel, into which Shadrach, Meshach and Abednego were thrown.

Also in the same area was a shallow oil well, where local Arabs or Kurds descended the few slippery black steps, filled skin containers, and loaded them onto donkeys to take them to a crude still outside the town. With the oil from this still I managed, during an emergency at the time of the Arab Revolt, to run a small oil engine generating electric light for the local British garrison. But the oil was so filthy that the piston of the engine had to be removed each day for cleaning.

On my visit to Tekrit in March, I arrived by train at 3.00 am and slept the rest of the night in an empty tent near the railway. I had a day in Tikrit with Lt. FitzGibbon and Lt. Finlayson, and dined with General Morris that evening, before catching the 3.00 am train for the 7-hour journey to Shergat. Finlayson showed me round our works at Shergat and Baiji (55 miles away), after which I caught the overnight train for the 12-hour journey back to Baghdad.

The longer train journeys were often made at night, and I occasionally enjoyed the luxury of a private saloon in which to sleep. Later in March, Colonels Butterworth, Mousley, Bridcut and I, took the night train to Qizil Robat to inspect the site for the proposed cantonment there, and to visit the ice plant at Quaraghan. Our car was put onto a flat-bed wagon, hitched to the train for the journey, so that we could drive back to Baghdad the following night.

That Easter weekend, I shared a carriage on the overnight train to Mosul with three others who were going on to Erbil. In the morning I left the train at Shergat, where Major Jordan met me in his new Mercedes, and we inspected our out-station there before driving on to Mosul for dinner, followed by bridge, with Mr and Mrs Marshall. On Easter Monday, 5th April, Jordan took me to see the pumping plant and the ice plant which required a new engine, and then we joined Col. Turner to visit the proposed site of the new cantonment.

There was some labour trouble at Quryarah which Jordan had to go and settle the following day – it was the beginning of the insurrection which came to a head as the full-scale Arab Revolt during the summer of 1920. I spent the day inspecting the stores and accounts, and had a difficult discussion with the storekeeper over some anomalies in the books. I turned in early that night, feeling unwell, and left early on Thursday morning; Jordan drove me back to Shergat where I boarded the train for the 186-mile journey to Baghdad, arriving at 5.45 am the next morning. I went straight to bed after a bath, and was taken to hospital in an ambulance that afternoon, 9th April. Malaria was common in the Quaraghan region of Mesopotamia, and I must have caught it on one of my earlier visits.

It was a week before my fever subsided and I felt comfortable and well enough to write a letter home, but it was not until Tuesday

20th, after 11 days in bed, that I got up and dressed for the first time. I had a visit from Col. Bridcut and Major Douglas, and wrote letters to half a dozen of my Canadian friends, but I was not discharged from hospital for another six days.

The Lion of Babylon statue in basalt

Ancient and modern modes of transport in the desert

Bedouins with an English officer near Ramadi

The Persian Lines of Communication – the road to Kasvin

An interesting side-line to my main duties in Mesopotamia was the completion of the 350 mile stretch of new road from Khanaquin, on the Mespot-Persian border, to Kasvin, not far from Tehran. The route had been selected extremely well by Russian engineers under General Denikin, and became the main route into Persia (Iran) from Iraq, crossing three mountain ranges over passes at elevations of 6,500ft to 7,700ft, all reached by a series of hair-pin bends. Our work involved widening and surfacing the track, and installing culverts and bridges where necessary; for this I had several detachments of Punjabis operating stone-crushers and road rollers along the route. When I visited any of our works, I would raise Cain if I found any of the men, Indians or Arabs, slacking. A certain amount of surplus labour at times was inevitable, but the climate, personal inclination, and surroundings, as well as cheap labour and supervision, all tended towards slack performance of duties.

After recovering from my fever, at the end of April I left on the evening train to Quraitu, for another visit to Kermanshah to inspect our work on the road. I had tiffin in Quraitu with the 1115th Mechanical Transport (MT) Company, before being driven in the Ford car to Karind, where I spent the night in the 65th Sappers & Miners camp once again. The 61-mile drive to Kermanshah the next morning was rough but uneventful, and I arrived in time for lunch with Alfred and Maude Tayler at the Accountant's House, staying with them for five nights.

Our Ford car on inspection of the road to Kasvin

From Kermanshah I joined Lt. Lane, my officer responsible for the Persian Lines of Communication, and we drove to Hamadan and Kasvin, inspecting the work along the way. We put up on the first night with the 64th Pioneers at Hamadan, and had a jolly evening with Col. Bliss and his officers, playing vingt-et-un after dinner. The usual car trouble en route delayed us somewhat, as did terrific storms and hail near Kasvin, where we stayed a couple of nights. We also found that our Model T Ford, which had only a gravity feed of petrol to the engine, had to be driven backwards up some of the steeper mountain passes with its petrol tank in front. After reaching the top of the first pass, our driver said that the brakes were insufficient to stop the car from accelerating downhill, so we had to drive down each pass in low gear for miles and miles!

In Kasvin I reported on the progress of our work to General Hugh Bateman-Champain, GOC North Persian Force, and Major McIntyre. On the return journey, Lane and I stopped and spent a day in Hamadan, visiting the bazaar where I paid 233/- Rupees for the first two of several Persian carpets I collected during my time in Mesopotamia. Almost 50 years later, they were still in good condition and in regular use, carpeting the rooms of our home in Wivenhoe. The list of carpets I bought, and their prices, may be of some interest to collectors:

	Rupees
Old blue Hamadan - large antique	200/–
Old brown Hamadan - cheap	33/–
Large Feraghan - 320 knots/sq.in - Jooshaghan design	200/–
Feraghan - red with lozenge design	70/–
Baktiari - with magenta centre field	60/–
Hamadan - antique dated 1260 (=1844) - soft camel hair	240/–
Bijar - large and strong	120/–
Bijar - nearly square	120/–
Kashan-Tabriz - tree of life design	250/–
Kerman - tree of life design	300/–
Jooshaghan - blue	250/–
Baluchistan	80/–
Feraghan - brown (1924 - Basra)	60/–
Herez - 10ft x 10ft	150/–
Sultanabad - Jooshaghan design - Shah Abbas pattern	150/–

(The exchange rate fluctuated but at that time £1 = Rps.10/-)

Mountain passes on the road
to Kasvin

My Staff in Mosul – 1920

The Arab Revolt - 1920

The Arab Revolt in 1920 caused me much anxiety, and a great deal of expense for the British Army; it dominated events for the rest of the year. The spread of the revolt throughout Mesopotamia required the reinforcement of the British Expeditionary Force by a division of troops from the Indian Army.

The unrest was caused by Arab nationalists frustrated at the lack of progress in establishing an Arab government in Iraq. Feisal, the son of Sharif Hussein, had been appointed by General Allenby, on the instructions of the British Government, as the new ruler in Syria, although that country would come within the sphere of influence of France following the Paris Peace Conference in 1919.

Negotiations between the French and British on how to divide up the Middle East had taken place as far back as 1916. The two men who led these negotiations were Sir Mark Sykes, a visionary British politician and Françoise George Picot, a French diplomat with a grudge.

The deal they struck, subsequently called the Sykes-Picot Agreement, carved the Arab territories of the collapsed Ottoman Empire into separate states on either side of an imaginary 'Line in the Sand' between Kirkuk in the north and Acre on the Mediterranean coast in what is now Palestine, the French having control of the area north of the line and the British having control in the south. The boundaries in the agreement were based for the most part on administrative arrangements which had existed under the Ottomans for hundreds of years but took more account of the European interests than those of the local populations concerned and contradicted the promises made by the British to the Arabs to give them self rule.

This was not what Feisal, the commander of the Arab Revolt, had been promised by T E Lawrence, his trusted British liaison, military and political adviser and friend.

Sharif Hussein, with his son Feisal, had helped the British to defeat the Turks and expected to be duly rewarded. He wished to create an Arab kingdom that included Arabia, Syria, Lebanon, Palestine, and Iraq. He wanted the throne of Hejaz, his Arabian turf, for himself, and he wanted two of his sons formally installed in the north: Feisal (already there) in Damascus, and his eldest son Abdullah, in Baghdad.

However, the British had made promises to the French as well as to Hussein and were caught in a compromising position. Negotiations at the Paris Peace Conference in 1919 between the two countries, with Feisal and Lawrence trying to exert their influence, became tortuous and the issues, deemed too difficult to settle, were deferred, in true diplomatic style, for two years.

Prior to the release of the Anglo-French Declaration of Arab liberation at the end of the war most Iraqis had accepted the idea their country would remain under direct British control. However, the declaration opened up other possibilities which were regarded with universal anxiety but gave opportunity for political intrigue to the less stable and more fanatical elements.

On one end of the tug-of-war stood the groups whose self-interests lay with the British. At the other end were the nationalists who wanted British forces withdrawn or overthrown so that the Arabs could rule themselves. In Damascus, Feisal had collected around him a group of nationalists, mostly of Mesopotamian origin, and was lobbying the British for support for independence for Mesopotamia under the rule of the Sharifian family.

Of those who identified with the British, the Naqib of Baghdad, the religious leader of the Sunnis, stood out as a wise and reliable friend. Although he refused to make any public political statements he believed the country was not yet ripe for any form of Arab rule. He emphasised the need for British troops to maintain the peace and hoped that a British administration would slowly incorporate Arabs into its government. However, even he *was nervous that the British might remain in control too long and he made a plea for Sir Percy Cox to be reassigned from his post of Ambassador in Persia, to return to Baghdad as the British High Commissioner in Iraq, where he was well known and trusted.*

The trouble erupted around Dair in the north, where the renegade Arab, Ramadhan al Shallash, had seized control and held British officers hostage in defiance of Feisal, declaring that the British had to withdraw their occupying forces fifty miles below their existing lines in Anah. He announced that he was also sending his forces farther north on the attack toward Mosul. He collected taxes inside British territory, sent threatening letters to the Political Officers and encouraged the tribes to rob and raid. In February 1920, he was replaced by Maulud al Khalaf, an even more prominent member of the nationalist Ahd al Iraqi and the situation became worse. Shiite holy men in Karbala and Najaf in the south had banded together with notables from Dair and Mosul in the north to incite rebellion against the British and, in early March 1920, they sent their representatives to an Arab Congress in Damascus.

The Arab Congress proclaimed Feisal King of Syria and, with his approval, the Mesopotamian representatives to the meeting pronounced his brother Abdullah, King of Iraq. This caused much alarm in the British Government and diplomatic circles where it was firmly believed that the Arabs could not govern themselves properly. However, Mesopotamia had already cost Britain too much money and too many lives. There were 17,000 British and 44,000 Indian troops in Iraq and, combined with the 23,000 troops in Palestine, it was costing England £35 million a year to keep the garrisons in place. This was the price of retaining Britain's important oil interests in the region. If Mesopotamia was lost, so then Persia and India may go also.

In the end a British commission was formed to seek a mandate from the League of Nations. At the Conference at San Remo in April 1920 an agreement was finally reached on the division of the Arab lands under the former Ottoman rule. Arabia would remain an independent peninsular, guided by the British; Syria, including Lebanon, would be mandated to France; Mesopotamia and Palestine would be mandated to Britain; in both cases until such time as they "could stand on their own".

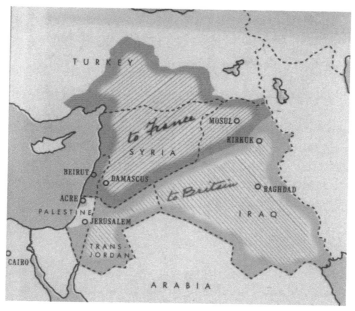

The map of the Middle East following the Sykes-Picot Agreement

The news reached Baghdad on May 1ˢᵗ 1920 together with a communiqué from Lt.Col. Arnold T Wilson, the British Resident in Baghdad, stating that the aim was "the creation of a healthy body politic," with Britain serving as "a wise and far-seeing guardian". Steps would be taken, he announced, to "prepare the way for creation of an independent Arab State of Iraq". But the British still refused to establish a constitution for Iraq until a peace treaty with Turkey had been signed.

At the end of May it was 100 degrees in Baghdad and the heat was becoming oppressive. The unrest boiled over and the Sunni townsmen and Shiite tribesmen put aside their bitter prejudices and joined together against the common enemy, the British, supported by gold from Turkish and extremist sources who wanted the infidel out of their country. When one young hothead made wild speeches, Frank Balfour, Governor of Baghdad, had him arrested, but this fuelled the fire. There were riots in the streets and a general strike was declared. The flare up was particularly annoying to the British troops who were not at their best in the heat, much preferring scrapping in winter.

I personally had many anxious days and nights after GHQ's secret service unit warned me that my Central Electricity Power Station, supplying the whole of Baghdad, was threatened. However, on the advice of my senior Arab employee, the superintendent of the ice plant, I did not obey their official order to dismiss all my Arab employees. He was confident that the risks would be greater if my Arab workmen were out of work and on the streets; fortunately, he was correct. I had a platoon of Indian soldiers on duty with a Lewis gun and a night guard of firewatchers on duty all night, to whom I used to pay periodic visits to check that all was well.

In June, Arnold Wilson spoke to the new army commander, General Sir Aylmer Haldane, and warned him that trouble was expected in the lower Euphrates. On 4th June at Tel Afar, forty miles west of Mosul, 2 officers and 14 other ranks were murdered. Wilson responded at once, ordering the areas to be machine-gunned, the insurgents imprisoned, their leaders deported and houses to be destroyed.

The British relied heavily on their long lines of communication for the transport of troops, ammunition, and stores. These were extremely vulnerable; it was impossible to adequately guard and defend the full length of 910 miles of roads, 856 miles of railways, and a similar length of waterways, against raids from bands of Arab rebels.

In an attempt to defuse the situation, Sir Percy Cox arrived in Baghdad from Tehran at the end of June. He approved a statement drafted by Wilson calling for a Constitutional Assembly and announced that Mesopotamia was to be made an independent state, under the guarantee of the League of Nations, and subject to the mandate of Great Britain.

The rebellion continued throughout August; four hundred British soldiers were attacked on a march and half were taken prisoner, Political Officers were ambushed, and a curfew was imposed in Baghdad. The Baghdad to Quraitu railway line was cut and Lt.Col. Gaskell, with his 65th battalion of Sappers & Miners, managed to drive off an attack on the bridge they were building on the road between Khanaquin and Qizil Robat.

In a letter to my sister in August, I wrote that 'Asquith's Government's lukewarm attitude to the British occupation does not help, and his speech strengthens the hands of our enemies and of those who want to kick us out.'

By September the rebellion had spread to the southern Euphrates where local tribes attacked a train, rescued prisoners, and cut the railway lines. When two hundred troops were sent in to help the stranded soldiers, the Arabs captured the armoured train and grabbed their guns.

Searchlight mounted on a railway flat-car and manned by Sikh's

At the height of the troubles I assisted General Atkinson's column which was advancing up the Euphrates valley to relieve Samarra, and provided him with a searchlight section manned by a few of my Sikh electricians who operated a searchlight and gun mounted on a railway flat-car. They became terribly frightened by the risk of attack from local tribesmen, and I had some difficulty in persuading them not to down tools and flee.

Sayid Talib, regarded by some as a spokesman for the nationalists, arrived in Baghdad and started to put together a moderate Arab party, for which he sought British support. This calmed the situation and by the end of the autumn the insurrection had quietened down. It had cost Britain £50 million and many British lives; several thousand Arabs had been killed.

Sir Percy & Lady Cox at his investiture in 1923

Sir Arnold Wilson was set to depart, and Sir Percy and Lady Cox arrived in Baghdad on 11th October 1920 amid great excitement and celebrations. In 1909 he and Wilson had negotiated a rental agreement on behalf of the British, for the island of Abadan, where large oilfields had been discovered the previous year, and the Anglo-Persian Oil Company was formed. Cox knew the Middle East well and had been the first British Ambassador to Tehran in 1918. He was respected by the Arabs and sympathetic to their plight.

His role, as the first High Commissioner under the Iraqi mandate, was to create an Iraqi Government in which the British influence was less visible. On 2nd November 1920, the Council of State of the first Arab Government in Mesopotamia since the thirteenth century Abbasids, met for the first time.

As part of the process of handing over to the Arabs, GHQ in Baghdad and the local representative of the British Treasury agreed with my suggestion that the electricity undertakings in Baghdad and Basra should be run on less military lines, and turned into quasi-Government, quasi-commercial undertakings, as a step towards their ultimate privatisation. I proposed the name of BESA which stood for the Baghdad (or Basra) Electricity Supply Authority, and this was adopted. These changes enabled us to eliminate a great deal of red tape and simplify the military procedures. For example, the military system had required 5 copies of each bill to be produced for even the smallest sale amounting to only 1 Rupee.

We set up a system to sell all electricity, water and ice, which was surplus to Army requirements, to the local civilian population who willingly paid one shilling a unit for both power and light. In this way I took nearly £100,000 per year over the counter, reducing the cost of support to the Army, and proving the valuable goodwill of the companies before their eventual sale by the British Government.

Furthermore, as each garrison was evacuated by the troops during the run-down of the British Army in Iraq, I had surplus plant, including electricity generating units, pumping systems and ice-making plants, to dismantle or sell to the local authority.

Whilst the revolt was underway during the summer months, I kept my visits to our various out-stations very short. I only spent one day at each of our facilities at Dewaniyeh, Hillah, Kingerbah, Kirkuk, Ramadi and Kut, returning to Baghdad overnight. During my visit to Dewaniyeh in June, I drew up an agreement with the local Political Officer to hand over to his Civil administration a complete new electric lighting system, which the E&M Section had installed in that small town, at a cost of about £6,000; it was to become the first of such plants not owned by the Military.

During a visit to Hillah on 1st September I noted that 'the 60 pounders of the garrison were busy in the afternoon.' My chief concern there was the stability of the 2 ton/day ice factory which the Military had hired from us until November. The water level on the Hillah branch of the river had risen, following the construction of a barrage at Hinaidi, and the building was water-logged and ready to collapse; I needed to keep it standing for a few more months.

Things were a bit quieter in October and I spent two weeks visiting our facilities in Basra, Nasiriyeh, and Kurnah, taking a goods train to Kut with Capt. Paynter King and then boarding the PA4 stern-wheeler to Amara, Kurnah and Basra. In Basra I stayed at the RE House, and was taken round the electricity and pumping stations with Inglis and Healey. On another two-week inspection trip at the end of October, I took the train to Quraitu, and went back to Hassanabad, Kermanshah, Hamadan, and Kasvin in Persia. At the end of November, I went north to the mainly Sunni cities of Samarra, Shergat, Tekrit and Mosul on my final inspection of 1920.

On 4th December I arranged for my Electrical and Mechanical Section in Bagdhad to hold a Sports Meeting. His Excellency the High Commissioner and Lady Cox and the GOC in Chief all accepted my invitation to attend our 'Sports and At Home', and Lady Cox agreed to present the prizes.

The Baghdad Times reported that: 'From the time the idea was first mooted by Lt.Col. Lott and a representative committee of British, Indian, and local employees was elected, everyone lent a willing hand to make the affair a huge success. Local interest in the Sports is undoubtedly intense and the friendly rivalry between departments is causing a great deal of fun. The E&M Section extends a hearty welcome to personnel of other Government departments and civilian employees to turn up and cheer their representatives to success.'

The day started 'promptly at 8 am' and included the following events:

100 yds and 400 yds
races
120 yds hurdles
High jump, Long jump &
Pole vault,
Bhisties race
Throwing the cricket ball
Wheel-barrow race
Sack race
Obstacle race
Tug of War
Slow cycle race
Mule race
Pillow fighting
One mile flat race
Veterans' race

Distribution of prizes at
4.15 pm
"God Save the King"

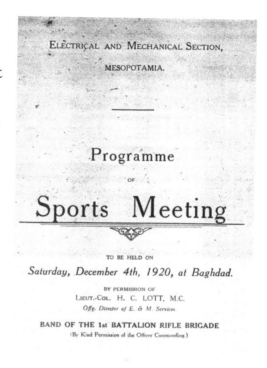

ELECTRICAL AND MECHANICAL SECTION,

MESOPOTAMIA.

Programme

OF

Sports   Meeting

TO BE HELD ON

Saturday, December 4th, 1920, at Baghdad.

BY PERMISSION OF
LIEUT.-COL. H. C. LOTT, M.C.
Offg. Director of E. & M. Services.

BAND OF THE 1st BATTALION RIFLE BRIGADE
(By Kind Permission of the Officer Commanding.)

The event was indeed a great success and so, after the usual Christmas celebrations, my first eventful year in Mesopotamia ended. I had well and truly settled in and become thoroughly familiar with the country and all my out-stations, with my Army and Government colleagues, and the men whom I employed. I also felt fitter than ever and full of life, after having a couple of septic tooth roots removed earlier in the year.

I had survived the summer in Baghdad without too much discomfort; the air was extraordinarily dry, and we had fans to provide a breeze in the office and the mess. Everyone had a siesta between 2 and 4 o'clock in the afternoon, and we drank plenty of liquid. I generally had several cups of tea a day and 15 bottles of mineral water (not so gassy as in England), only adding a little alcohol in the evenings.

On 30ᵗʰ December I wrote to Col. A.B. Carey CMG DSO RE, who had taken over as Chief Engineer, informing him that:

"My contract term of service was completed yesterday. Not having received any orders to hand over my duties, I am continuing to carry them out, but would like a written assurance from you:
a) that additional service is required of me;
b) that I shall receive 3 months' notice if no longer required;
c) that the provisional offer of normal increment which you verbally authorised me to make to my time expired officers, applies also in my case; and
d) that in other matters the terms of the present contract will hold until modified by a revised agreement.

"It is essential for family reasons that I return to England for my furlough, leaving Basra at the end of March or in the first week in April. As the time for booking a passage is already short, may I have your early written approval for this as Lt.Col. Bridcut is not back in this country until March."

Col. Carey immediately signed a further one-year contract for me at the rate of Rps.1,650 per month, a small increment of only Rps.50. In response to my claim, a total of £520.15s.6d was remitted to my agents, to cover my furlough pay since departure from England in September 1919 and my passage to and from England.

During the year I had saved almost half my salary, sending remittances to London amounting to Rps.7,265, equivalent to £780 at an average of 2s.2d per rupee (the value of sterling during the year had halved from 1s.5d. to 2s.9d. per rupee). I also sent Rps.1,500 to my account with Cox & Co in Bombay. With the assistance of their stock department I invested my savings in War

Savings Certs, £300 in 4% Funding Loan, £100 in 5% Exchequer Bonds, and £300 in 5% NW Bonds. Together with my 30 shares in Imperial Bank of Persia and $500 in 6% Wayagamack (Canadian) Bonds, my total investments amounted to £1,300, plus £935 cash in various accounts, making my net worth just £2,235.

My Staff in Baghdad – 1921

Baghdad in 1921

The year 1921 began with my acting as Director of Electrical & Mechanical Services Mesopotamia and North-West Persia, in the absence on furlough of my boss, Lt.Col. Bridcut. Although I received a small increase in pay for the additional duties, I could have done without the added responsibility. The weather in January was like spring in England, with some drizzle but generally sunny and sometimes even cold.

Living with me in our mess, 'The Work House' in River Street, were Lt.Col. A.B. Carey, CMG DSO (Chief Engineer), Lt.Col. J.H. Mousley DSO (Assistant Director Works), Major H.H. Wheatley OBE MC, Lt.Col. W.B. Lane CBE (Director of Health Services, Civil), Capt. Todd (11th Hussars) and Major E.G. Henderson. To the inquisitive looking at the hanging sign outside, we said that it was where the real workers lived!

After dinner in the evenings, Wheatley, Mousley and I would play bridge with one or two of the other officers; we played for small stakes, and my diary notes that after one evening I lost 2 rubbers, 14 points, Rps. 7/-, and on another occasion, 'have most successful evening at bridge, Rps. 15/-'. I had bought a piano for the Work House on which I practised and played for our guests on musical evenings. Occasionally we would go to see a film in a nearby cinema; 'Tarzan and the Apes' was on one day when we saw Lady Cox there in a box with friends.

We had guest nights once a week to which ladies were sometimes invited; mostly officers' wives and one or two nurses from the military or civil hospitals: Miss Iles, Miss Wilson, Miss Barnaby, or Miss Hawkins. After dinner, the ladies would go into the anteroom, separated from the mess room by a curtain, and the men would join them a quarter of an hour later for cards. I was occasionally anti-social and escaped to my room after dinner to write letters and turn in early. I used to get up at 5.00 am to be in the office by 6.45 am, and needed 6 hours sleep. Sometimes there was dancing after dinner, and the ladies turned up in elaborate evening gowns whilst the men were in their khaki uniform. The Indian servants all wore white, with red and blue sashes, and a similar band of colour in their turbans or 'puggarees'.

The menus were formidable and normally started with hors d'oeuvres, followed by a soup, and then a fish course, which was generally Tigris 'salmon', a coarse white fish with bones in all directions! After that we had an entrée, meat or game, and a sweet dish, followed by a savoury and finally dessert. The port for the loyal toast was followed by coffee and liqueurs, and later by unlimited whiskies and soda; and there were always plenty of roasted and salted almonds and monkey nuts with the drinks. The Indian cook's spelling was somewhat quaint, and I retained a copy of the menu for one of the guest evenings at a junior mess in Baghdad which read:

Stuffard Olives and Sadine
Clear Muck Tortoise Soup
Boiled Fish and allandan sauce *(Hollandaise sauce)*
Compet Pegion and Haspic
Roast Geese & Tamarind Sauce,
apple, potatoes, carlic flower & peas
Savery Icet Palagrass *(asparagus!)*
Boiled Plum Pudding hasbrigade sauce
Cold porched Eggs pudding
Coffee & Deserse

The cooks excelled in making the dishes attractive, and amongst their many elaborate sweets was one of my favourite dishes - an intricately woven basket made of clear toffee, containing a fruit salad. In helping oneself, one broke off a section of the brittle yellow toffee basket to eat with the fruit. It always seemed a shame to destroy such a work of art.

The Sikh festival of Lodhi was celebrated on Sunday 16th January, and, with several of my officers, I attended the main event around a bonfire in our Indian camp where many hundreds were present. I made a short speech in response to their thanks to the British Officers, after which we were all entertained to refreshments.

The next day I received alarmist telegrams from Basra and decided to make a visit there before the end of January. The train to Kut was 'only' 8 hours late, but I had time to visit the local plants there, including the south end pumping station, before spending the night in the E&M bungalow. I was allotted a passage on the paddle-steamer PS 60 which set off the next morning with the usual two barges, one on either side.

Tigris river paddle-steamer accompanied by two barges

During the seven-hour stop at Amara I met Capt. Paynter King, and we visited the left bank power station, the Pindi Point pumping station, and the resources wharf, returning to my cabin for a drink before we departed. On arrival in Basra, Mr Hooper of Hill Bros. kindly gave me, my servant, and my kit, a lift to RE House, where I had a chat with the Jobsons before turning in. The next day, Lt.Col. Jobson took me in his car to see the power station, with its leaning chimney and broken alternator shaft, then to see the bad foundations for the 300 ton elevated water tower.

During a week in Basra I met with Col. Ward, the Port Director, to negotiate the terms of the electricity supply to the cranes at the Port, based on 5 annas per unit, and visited Gen. Nepean and Col. Powell AQMG to discuss the necessity for much greater economy in the use of electricity at the Base. I also discussed the shutting down of the IWT (Inland Water Transport) ice plant, and my proposal for taking over the stationary barges.

Visits to Mespers (the Mesopotamia Persia Corporation), the Civil Base Depot, and to Makina and Ashar to find Major Kiermander, AD Railways, were not very productive, but on a second visit to Makina Station with Lt.Col. Jobson and Capt. F.C. Inglis, we met Lt. Mills of Mesopotamian Railways, and he took us in a tractor to Shaiba station, enabling us to inspect the new pipeline on the way.

On 29th January Jobson and I crossed the river in a launch and took two cars, one following with the luggage, to drive to Ahwaz. However, it was raining hard, and we only got 22 miles before the flat, apparently limitless desert, became impassable, and we had to turn back. Back in Basra I spent time in the office, the workshops and stores, and had discussions with Jobson and D.L. Morgan on the budget and establishment for the next financial year.

On my return journey up the Tigris to Kut, I met Paynter King again at Amara, and stopped briefly at Aligharbi to look at pumping station A, which threatened to collapse into the river, and pumping station B, which was nearly dismantled. In Kut I saw the new municipal power plant start up, and inspected the distribution system and the local plants in the Kut cantonment, but 'had no sleep on the train to Baghdad, having been fixed up for the night in a smelly horse-truck'.

Back in the Work House on 6th February, I found that the mess had been reduced to four officers. However, the following week, Capt. Butler took over Todd's job and Col. Turner (Conkey Bill) arrived from England. Later, we were joined by Lt. Grand RE, who was prepared to take over the messing from Major Wheatley when he moved to the suburb of Alwiyah, where the Alwiyah Club had just opened. Alwiyah had become the centre of the British community in Baghdad, and was where Agatha Christie stayed in 1928 when she wrote 'Murder in Mesopotamia'. The Iraqi capital being all the rage in Britain at the time, she had come out to obtain new material for her novels, and to experience life in the Middle East.

During February and March I spent most of the time in Baghdad, dealing with administration in the office, checking on progress at the new cantonment we were building at Hinaidi, seeing the new 120 hp Ruston engine commissioned in the left bank pumping station, and visiting our other facilities, including the dairy farms and the Baghdad north filtration plant.

Summer Leave 1921

On 23rd March I left Baghdad with Mousley to go on leave, and handed over my duties to Regular Army officer Lt.Col. F.W. Robertson. We caught the train to Kut, taking with us my bearer Samuel and Peter, the senior Chaldean bath-boy from the Work House mess. On arrival in Kut we spent the day in the town, and stayed the night with T.H. Andrews in his bungalow. The next morning C.E. Capito drove us 74 miles to the camp at Aligharbi, to inspect the works, and then four of us went out with shotguns, bagging 20 sand grouse, 1 quail and a fox. After dinner we boarded the PS 59 which had arrived from Kut, and went down-river to Amara and Basra, where we had booked a passage to Bombay on the S.S. Varela.

The S.S. Varela had been built in 1914 by Swan Hunter in Newcastle, especially for the Bombay - Persian Gulf run. It had been commandeered during the War as a hospital ship, but it was now back in service with the British India Line. On 28th March, after saying our farewells in Basra, Mousley and I boarded the Varela and shared a cabin, arriving in Bombay 6 days later, after a relatively smooth voyage across the Gulf of Oman and the Indian Ocean.

S.S.Varela

As we had a week in India before leaving for England on the S.S. Caledonia, Mousley and I took the train to Agra, stayed a couple of nights in Lauries Great Northern Hotel, and hired a guide to show us round the Taj Mahal, Agra Fort and Fatephur Sikri. In Bombay I went to the Eagle Star Insurance Company to insure my kit and carpets, paying £4.19.0 for £440 cover. After tea and a chat with Dearing at the Taj Mahal Hotel one evening, I changed into a dinner suit to dine with Major J.H.K. Douglas at the Royal Bombay Yacht Club.

On Sunday 10th April, I spent 'a very strenuous, hot, and sticky morning packing, and getting cabin baggage through the check-weighers, and onto the ship. We finally boarded at 11.00 am, after a tiresome delay for a perfunctory medical examination and passport check, and left Ballard Pier at 3.15 pm.' The Caledonia was an old, but fast, single screw vessel built in 1894; it was scrapped in Bombay in 1925, when the name was given to a newly built S.S. Caledonia (the third).

One of the several interesting people on board was Rosita Forbes, an early English traveller in the region, who pretended to be an Arab woman when she visited the Kufra oasis in the Sahara in 1921. Apart from Mousley, my table companions during the relatively uneventful voyage included two nursing sisters, Miss Spence and Miss Barton, Dr and Mrs (Dr) Sinderson, Major Pulley (from Hillah), Capt. Wright, Lt.Col. J.N. Metcalfe, and Major E.B. Soane CBE. Dr (later Sir Harry) Sinderson, had been working as a surgeon in Baghdad and Hillah; he was appointed doctor to Feisal and the Iraqi Royal Family and Dean of the College of Medicine in Baghdad in 1923.

Soane was another interesting character, who knew (and loved) the Kurds better than any European. He wrote about his travels in Kurdistan in 1909 disguised as a Persian, when he stayed at the court of the Lady of Halabja, whom he used to delight with his skilful reading of Persian poetry. His knowledge of the Kurdish language and Kurdish people was unrivalled; he described them as "shedders of blood .. robbers and brigands .. malignant and evil doers of depraved habits .. brave and fearless .. of a hospitality grateful to the soul .. in truth and honour unequalled .. of pleasing countenance and fair cheek .. boasting of all the goods of beauty and grace. What a wealth of paradox!" He insisted on Kurdish being spoken in his Division, but received little encouragement in his policy of creating a Kurdish nation, and was working on an etymological survey of the Kurdish language when he died prematurely later in 1921.

We docked in Marseilles on 24th April, and Mousley and I immediately transferred to the special train which took us to Paris and Boulogne. We arrived in Dover on the steamer Invicta at 2.30 pm the following day, and caught the P&O Pullman to London, staying at the Grosvenor Hotel that night, before going our separate ways.

Having escaped the worst of the summer heat in Baghdad, I enjoyed three months leave in England, before returning to

Marseilles and boarding the S.S. Sicilia for Bombay on 30th July. During those three months I based myself with my parents who were then living in Holbrook, having had to give up Wenham Place Farm when it was sold by the owner to a wealthy American. Apart from the usual visits to my cousins, aunts, and friends in the nearby villages, and to my sister Clara in her new home in Mistley, I went up to London on several occasions, to a dentist in Harley Street to have a new set of upper dentures fitted. The cost of £19.19.0 was slightly reduced by the credit of £2.5.0 for the value of the gold in my old plate!

In London, I visited Cyril and Mrs Skinner and, of course, my sister May and her family in Harrow on the Hill. My brother Charlie came down from Lincolnshire, and he and I spent several days by the sea at the Grand Hotel in Clacton, before we went north to his home in Kirton. I spent a week there with his family, followed by a week based at the Caledonian Hotel in Edinburgh, meeting my Canadian friend J.M. Crabbe, visiting his office at Balfour Beatty & Co., and travelling around Scotland with him, before returning home via Liverpool and spending a couple of nights with Arthur Atkins' family.

S.S. Sicilia

I left England on 29th July on the P&O train from Victoria, arriving in Marseilles the following day. There I boarded the S.S. Sicilia which, at 6,700 tons and 4,500 hp, was the smallest and slowest of the P&O liners on the India run and carried only about 160 passengers. Built in 1900 and scrapped in 1926, it was used as a troopship during the War. The somewhat uncomfortable voyage from Marseilles to Bombay took 17 days.

Four of my ten days in India I spent on a trip to Delhi, almost 900 miles away, to see the progress on the construction of Lutyens' New Delhi and visit the waterworks. In Bombay I stayed at the Taj Mahal Hotel, and met up with colleagues including Livingstone Learmonth, Major L.S. Harris, Lt.Col. Butterworth, and Major P.D. Low, before Mousley and I boarded the S.S. Varela on 26th August for the voyage back to Basra. The ship rolled heavily in the Indian Ocean and I felt miserable, despite taking Mothersill's Seasickness Remedy daily.

Back in Baghdad – Autumn 1921

On my arrival in Basra on 2nd September it was guest night at the RE House, and I was able to catch up with Inglis, Morgan, and several others. We visited Shaiba to see the new cantonment and RAF buildings, the Mespers office, the ice plant and power house, before catching the train to Baghdad. The journey took 30 hours over two nights and a day, but it was better than having to take the river steamer to Kut. There was some excitement during the night involving an Arab train robber but, alas, my automatic pistol was unloaded at the time.

Mousley and I returned to the Work House where I had my old room, and resumed my original position as Deputy Director of E&M Services, reporting to Lt.Col. F.W. Robertson OBE, who, as Assistant Chief Engineer, was my new chief. Baghdad was still fearfully hot in September, with daytime temperatures up to 116 degrees, only dropping to 82 degrees at night. Whenever possible, I visited our facilities in the early morning or after siesta in the afternoon. There was trouble with the dairy farms' pumping plant, which I found in an appalling condition with only one barge pump running. At Hinaidi cantonment we took over the substation and installed a raw water irrigation plant. I also had work to do on the water supply at the Residency for Sir Percy and Lady Cox, and was, for a time, a member of the Baghdad City Council, responsible for designing an extension to the city's drinking water supply from the River Tigris.

With Lt.Col. Mousley in Baghdad

Shooting Parties

However, it was not all work and no play, and from mid-September onwards, Mousley and I went on several shooting trips to Bawi, Ctesiphon, Diata, Cassel's Post, Serai, Chaldari and elsewhere. For these we hired, either a Government launch for trips down the Tigris, or a railway coach or two freight box cars for shoots in the Baqubah area; one of the box cars being for the servants. The coaches or box cars would be shunted into a siding on the Saturday night, and picked up for the return journey to Baghdad the following night, leaving us the Sunday for our day shooting duck on the river, or sand-grouse and partridge in the desert. Sand-grouse, although gradually becoming scarcer, would sometimes rise in such numbers that one was tempted to fire at the flock, rather than an individual bird.

On one such trip in December, Mousley and I joined Col. Hunt DDVS and Capt. Knowles on an outing to the desert, west of Baghdad. We left in two trucks and were detached from the Hillah train at Khan Mahawil at 2.00 am. The weather was mild and the temperature a comfortable 63 degrees. After an early breakfast of hot (tinned) herrings in tomato sauce, eggs, bacon, and marmalade, at which I acted as maître d'hôtel, we set off, each selecting 2 Arab youths as beaters for 1 rupee each, and tramped about 15 miles in 7 hours, shooting 10 brace of black partridge, a curlew, and a hare! After returning to the trucks for tiffin of cold partridge, tinned meat, fruit, and cheese, we set off again, past many homesteads with noisy dogs, and returned by 3.30 pm to be picked up by the train on its way back from Hillah.

Hired railway transport for grouse and partridge shooting (weekend) trips from Baghdad into the desert near Baqubah

A week later, just before Christmas, I was invited to join Col. Hunt again, with two others, on a weekend shooting trip to Abu Gisrah. I took two Indians with me as beaters or pickers-up, and we boarded a special ambulance truck at Baghdad North station, arriving at Abu Gisrah in the early hours.

After breakfast, we walked through the village and picked up some Arab youths, wearing nothing much in the way of clothes, and found our way through the morning fog to the big jheel (lake or marsh). When we arrived at the shore the mist had lifted, and we realised we had missed our best chances. With ducks it was hard to approach sufficiently close without disturbing them. When disturbed in the early morning, the thousands of birds rising from the water made a tremendous noise, reminding me of the noise of the Atlantic rollers breaking on Chesil Beach in Dorset. Nevertheless, after several hours standing over our knees in water, we bagged a total of about 80 birds, including 60 duck, several partridges, a few snipe, and one goose. Very tired and hungry, we trudged back to our coach/shooting box soaked to our waist, and paid the local boys Rps.1/8, and the Indians Rps.2/8 each. The train was late picking us up, and we did not leave the siding until 4.30 am the next morning, getting into Baghdad 6 hours later.

Returning from a shoot on the Tigris
with Samuel, my bearer, in the white shirt on my left

Shooting parties - 1921

lt to rt: Lt. J.B.Glubb RE, Arab Sheikh, Lt. L.D.Grand RE,
Lt.Col. J.H.Mousley DSO

Heavy Oil Springs at Qaiyarah

I visited Qaiyarah during a trip to Shergat and Mosul with Col. Carey and Lt.Col. Rothera (CE of Railways) at the beginning of November. We had workshops and stores in Mosul and a pumping station and power house serving the RAF squadron based there. We also managed the operation of the crude oil wells at Qaiyarah, only a few miles from Mosul. These were experimental bores, drilled by the Germans, which had surprisingly been left intact when their allies the Turks retreated before the British forces in 1918. The wells were 8" and 12" in diameter and the pipes projected about 2 ft. above the ground. Oil filled them to the brim, and a little 'tickling' with a pencil as a stirrer, would excite the gases below and make them overflow with oil for a few minutes.

By lowering a sand-pump we obtained a flow of oil lasting an hour or so. The few barrels a day of oil we obtained in this way, we distilled in a crude still, also left by the Germans, and produced a filthy smelling paraffin on which my clever engineer, Major Jordan, succeeded in running 15 horizontal internal combustion engines, driving water and ice plants. The lighter distillate was discarded, as even the Arab lorry drivers found it useless for their lorries, and we used the heavy residue to help surface our dusty roads. Unfortunately, I was not allowed to drive the wells any deeper, in case I struck a gusher and flooded the valley with oil!

Jordan's Mercedes breaks down near Mosul

Our convoy of cars on the road to Mosul

After visiting our facilities in Mosul and Qaiyarah, and meeting with Col. Saunders and Major Gaskell, I had a day out in Slater's new car, driving 20 miles south in the Nineveh plains to Nimrud, to see the ruins of that ancient Assyrian city which Ashurbanipal II (883-859 BC) had made his capital.

The Tigris river-front near the Work House on River Street

Strong winds and torrential rainstorms flooded River Street on several occasions in November, leaving the street indescribably dirty and interrupting our weekend shooting trips.

Armistice Day, 11th November, was a holiday, and I went with Mousley to Khadiman station, and thence to Akkar Kuf (Aqar Quf) to see the ziggurat of Dur-Kurigalzu (14th Century BC). It was an impressive structure of sun-dried square bricks with reed mats laid every 7 layers for

Ziggurat of Dur-Kurigalzu

drainage. For desert travellers it used to be a sign that they were nearing Baghdad, and more recently it became a favourite place for Friday picnics.

In December we were notified by Col. Carey that the RE Services was to be reorganised in April, and brought under the RAF or the Colonial Office. There would be some reductions in the establishment, and we were all asked if we would continue to serve under the new organisation. In my case, Carey asked if I would mind being transferred to Basra as Deputy Director of Works and Deputy Director E&M Services. I agreed to accept, though of course the move was distasteful as the climate in Basra was much more oppressive.

So I spent the first week of January obtaining as much information as I could about the work of the RE Services in Basra, handing over my present responsibilities, and packing up my kit and my piano. After saying farewell to my friends and colleagues, I left for Basra on the train at 10.30 pm on 7th January 1922. On the way, I spent a day in Nasiriyeh with Lt. E.H. White, visiting the cantonment and the various E&M activities which would become part of my responsibilities, and arrived in Basra 57 hours after leaving Baghdad.

The Creek and Date Gardens near Baghdad

Transfer to Basra - 1922
Deputy Director of RE Services - Senior Works Officer

I arrived in Basra on 10th January to take over from Lt.Col. G.M. Gordon of the Norfolk Regiment, who was returning to England. My responsibilities, which I combined under the title Deputy Director of RE Services, covered an area which extended as far north as Amara on the Tigris and Nasiriyeh on the Euphrates. My employees included 2,920 enrolled Indians and 500 enrolled Persians, besides several hundred daily Arab labourers.

One of the first visits I made in my new position was to go with Lt. Howarth to the Maqil brickfields, where the moulded bricks were not drying, due to the cold weather; the temperature in January was a maximum of 70 deg. and went down to 60 deg. at night. We also made visits to the blockhouses which the 69th Sappers and Miners were constructing, to inspect the site for a new hospital, and to the Mesopotamian Railways office to discuss the level and diamond crossings. During the following days, with Lt.Col. R.H.T. Jobson and Lt. Inglis, I visited the pumping stations, the sub-stations, and the remains of the aerodrome, and met the Port Director to discuss arrangements for the transfer of Port Lands.

Brick making at the Maqil brickfields, Basra

I was warned that we would soon be required to reduce the No.1 Works Company by 500 men, and so, before he left, Lt.Col. Gordon and I went to GHQ Representative Base to meet with Lt.Col. Powell, Major Parrott, Capt. Dunford and Lt.Col. Hailmer, to review our activities at Amara and Nasiriyeh and the situation with our guards. A few days later, Lt. and Mrs Howarth left Basra for a permanent appointment in Jodhpur State, after a splendid send-off at a Garden Party, with a tennis tournament arranged for them by the RE Services.

We had, of course, no regimental silver so, realising that I would have to do some serious entertaining, I ordered from London two canteens of silver plated spoons, forks, and cutlery, four condiment sets, and some table cloths and napkins, at a total cost of £31.18s.7d. They arrived at the end of January, just in time for guest night on Monday 6th February, when I entertained at my own table for the first time in my life! Thus, I was able to have my end of the table well equipped for my principal guests who, on this occasion, were Lt.Col. F.W. Robertson, Mrs Kiernander, Lt. J.B. Gunhill and Mr Carson. On such guest nights my officers and I provided several Persian rugs and brasses from our sleeping quarters to adorn the Mess. The silver, inscribed with my initials, remains in use in the family today.

A few days later my dinner guest was Lt.Col. Smith of the Imperial War Graves Commission, who was visiting in order to establish a new 'peace' cemetery in the area. After dinner 'whilst jolly music went on downstairs, Smith, Jobson, Keenan and I played bridge in my room.' We normally played bridge after dinner and sometimes 'had a little music'.

There was a Ladies' Guest Night before Lt.Col. Gordon departed, to which we invited his fiancée as well as the Matron-in-Chief of the hospital, Miss Hoardley, Miss (Dr) Pfeil and some nursing sisters, and we all went on to the Makina Club where there was dancing after dinner. On Sunday afternoons Col. and Mrs Ward would sometimes invite us for tea and tennis on their lawn.

Towards the end of February, over a lunch at Shick Scott's, T.L. Jacks of the Anglo-Persian Oil Company (APOC) offered me a 3-year contract at a starting salary of £400/year plus Rps.5,400, with an annual increment of £20 and Rps.300. I gave it some thought but declined the offer, not really wanting to commit to several more years working in the region.

Amongst our larger projects in Basra was the No.3 British General Hospital (BGH) being built in the grounds of Sheikh Muhammarah's palace on Ashar Creek. On one of my visits to Ashar to meet Wilson, who was in charge of the project, I was very critical of the supervision of the work, condemning the method of bituminising the concrete.

Ashar Creek – Basra

One Saturday in February, after a walk around the old Hyde Park Ammunition Dump before breakfast, I met with Lt.Col. McMurray, Deputy Director of the Inland Water Transport (IWT) branch of the Corps of Royal Engineers, to discuss the building of the IWT Headquarters on the River Front.

I had lunch there as the guest of Col. Commandant Hamer and Lieutenant General (later Sir Edward) Bulfin; Col. Keogh and Lt.Col. Radcliffe were also present. Bulfin had a distinguished war record and proudly wore his three rows of medals with six foreign decorations!

Tigris river-steamer with two barges between Basra and Amara

Ezra's Tomb

At the end of February I received a telegram asking me to go to Amara, and I left that night with Holland on the IWT M87 launch for the 132 mile trip. We travelled overnight at about 6 miles/hour upstream against the current, catching up two steamers on the way, and reached Ezra's Tomb at 6.00 am having covered the 75 miles in 12 hours. We passed Qalat Saleh, reaching Amara at 4.30 pm after almost 24 hrs in the launch, and put up for two nights in Dobell's bungalow. C.H. Dobell was Deputy Director RE Services in Amara; he introduced us to Capt. Laycock, the Graves Registration Officer, and showed us round the cantonment and cemetery, the power house, the filtration plant, and the cotton press.

I was only back in Basra for a day before I had to leave by train for Baghdad, sharing a carriage with Major J.M. Wilson, Director of Public Works, to meet with Col. Carey, the Chief

Engineer. We had lunch in a dining car at Samawah, and dinner in a tent at Dewaniyeh, arriving in Baghdad at 6 am the following morning. In Baghdad, Carey and I visited the Hinaidi cantonment to look at the progress of the various works being built for the RAF.

By the end of March it was already getting hot, and the thermometer hit 99.5 degrees in the shade, but that did not stop us going to a dance at the Makina Club given by some other bachelors whose motto was 'nil desperandum'. However, it was not long before I was in hospital with a temperature of 101 degs. and a very swollen face. Fortunately, I was only there a week, during which time I received several visitors and had time to catch up with my correspondence, writing 20 letters to friends and relatives in the UK and Canada.

RAF Iraq Command

As part of the defence cuts after World War I, the newly formed RAF took up the task of policing the Empire from the air. In January 1921, the Mesopotamian Group of the RAF was formed and Churchill, then Colonial Secretary, agreed with the service chiefs that British forces in Iraq would be put under RAF control.

After Feisal's appointment as King of Iraq in August 1921, Churchill asked Hugh Trenchard, Chief of the Air Staff, for a cheaper alternative plan for air power to control Iraq rather than providing the extra land forces requested by the Army. He told Parliament he would reduce the British garrisons in Iraq from 33 to 23 battalions and cut expenditures by £5 million the first year and by £12 million the next. The RAF Iraq Command was formed the following year on 1st October 1922 under Air Marshall J M Salmond.

On 1st April 1922, responsibility for the RE Services was transferred from the Army Command to the RAF, my position was renamed Senior Works Officer, and I was given a Vauxhall in place of my unreliable Ford. We were working on several projects for the RAF, including their new base and hospital in Hinaidi and their HQ, barracks, hospital and rest camp in Basra. I was dealing with Majors Thomas and Watkins and Flight Lieutenant Woollett and entertained them to dinner, with bridge and music afterwards.

My car and driver in Basra with some local boys

Freemasonry

On 3rd July 1922 I was initiated as First Degree Freemason in the Basra Lodge. That afternoon I wrote to my sister Clara saying 'I am going to be a Mason and am attending the initiation meeting tonight. I have not the foggiest notion of what it means yet, nor shall I be able to tell you when I do know more about it. As I think Charlie found in India, it is supposed to be a great advantage to be a Mason, especially in the East. The reason is quite unknown to me.' I passed my Second Degree in Freemasonry on 16th August and was raised to Master Mason on 13th September. My assistant Morgan and Capt. Morris were both Masons and we attended most meetings together. At 'Lodge Babylonia' meetings, I was appointed Organist and was invited to dine as a guest of E.D.A. Bagot, the Worshipful Master, at his Installation Banquet in November 1923.

The Summer of 1922 in Basra

The climate in Baghdad had been on the whole delightful, except in the summer when a temperature of 115 degrees in the shade was not uncommon. The air was so dry, however, that this was far more endurable than summer in Bombay, when the temperature was 95 degrees and the humidity close to 100 per cent.

The shade temperature in Basrah on Tuesday was *125·3 DEGREES* 1922 which is probably a record for the month of May. Tuesday was an exceptionally unpleasant and humid day. Throughout the night the temperature did not fall below 80 degrees. We continue below our temperature comparisons with the corresponding period of last year:—

	1921.		1922.	
May.	Max.	Min.	Max.	Min.
24	112·3	79·6	108·7	77·4
25	113·2	84·8	107·3	81·4
26	113·2	84·8	107·7	79·4
27	109·3	84·0	108·9	80·1
28	106·7	80·5	116·4	73·8
29	112·9	80·4	105·0	79·7
30	111·8	80·5	115·6	80·4
31	118·9	87·8	123·3	80·0
Averages ...	112·3	82·8	111·6	79·2

However, Basra was more humid, and, during the summer of 1921, a shade temperature of 131 degrees had been recorded. The *average* daily maximum temperature that July had been 121 deg. It had still been 116 deg. in August, whilst average night-time minimums were 86 deg. in July and 82 deg. in August. Many died from heat-stroke, including six British soldiers who were sleeping under a fan in a barrack room. The quantity of beer or 'arak' which they had drunk the previous evening was probably a contributory cause. I was lucky to be in England on leave during that summer, although even England suffered from three months drought. Most weeks I included a cutting of the local temperature in my diary.

Each afternoon we had a siesta and snoozed for a couple of hours before going out again. When the heat in Basra became unbearable it was as if the city was smothered under a heavy, wet wool blanket, and I almost always took to the roof-top to sleep. Outdoors in the middle of the night I still awoke to find myself lying in a pool of sweat. Everything one touched was hot, all the inanimate objects, your hair, the biscuits you ate and the clothes you put on; malaria and typhoid were common.

Even in March the temperatures were unusually high, and, when the rains came to cool the air and lower the humidity, the city became coated with mud. After the rains had subsided, it felt fresher again and flowers appeared and created a burst of glory in April.

July 1921/22

1922   THURSDAY 20   JULY

• • •

This is surely "St. Martin's summer —halcyon days." The following comparisons are pleasant reading, despite the upward tendency the mercury has been showing during the last two or three days :—

	1921.		1922.	
July.	Max.	Min.	Max.	Min.
13	127·0	88·4	109·8	79·8
14	126·6	87·2	107·8	77·0
15	128·7	87·6	108·4	78·4
16	127·4	87·3	110·0	83·8
17	128·9	86·4	108·3	79·4
18	127·8	86·9	112·8	78·0
19	125·0	87·6	118·8	79·2
20	126·1	88·2	115·7	88·0
Averages ...	127·2	87·4	111·4	80·4

By the end of May 1922, the mercury rose to 123 degrees and remained high for months, reaching 125 degrees at the end of July. The excessive summer heat meant that travelling for several days, especially by rail, was almost intolerable. When I went to Amara, which I had to do on several occasions, I took the launch and slept on the deck if there were no mosquitoes. However, on 8th July, I succumbed to another bout of malaria and was taken into the Military Hospital in Basra with fever and abdominal pains. I was released 6 days later, just before my 39th birthday.

Autumn 1922

In October I was in Baghdad for a week of meetings with Col. Carey and stayed at the mess at White Lodge. During that week Carey and I visited Hinaidi to inspect the power house B, the filtration plant (30-40,000 gals/hour) and raw water plant, the central pool garage, and the accommodation which we were building for the RAF squadrons.

At the weekend, with my colleagues from the mess, Mousley, Edmonds, Bardon and Grand, we went by launch on a shooting trip down-river past Ctesiphon and landed on a sand island in mid-stream for the night. After an early morning walk on the mainland through low scrub of liquorice and tamarisk, we had breakfast on the launch, and then took up our position in butts on the island. In the four hours from 9 am until 1 pm we bagged 33 sand grouse, of which Grand shot 16 and I shot 8, plus 2 partridges and a rabbit. After lunch, we visited and photographed Ctesiphon before returning to Hinaidi for a bath and dinner at White Lodge.

At the end of another inspection visit by launch from Basra to Kurnah, Amara and Qalat Saleh, we had a weekend's shooting near the Maji Kabir irrigation barrage, and delivered 53 partridges and 8 quail to No 9 wharf on our return. I was with Bardon who 'only walked at 1 mile per hour and required his beater or bearer to bring a ramrod every time he fired a shot'!

Back in Basra on 16th October we had our last dinner before moving our mess to a new RE House. I had a serious talk with the Senior Medical Officer about the site for the new RAF rest camp, and got approval for the sites of the new operating theatre, dispensary and drug store, dental rooms, ophthalmic room, heat stroke wards, laboratory annex, and BOR's quarters and mess. Afterwards we invited Lt.Col. Graham (Inspector General of Civil Health Services) to dinner with Dr Hall, Miss (Dr) Pfeil, Capt. France and Miss Hatton.

November was the month for writing my Christmas letters. I ordered five cases of wine as presents for the family through the Times Supply Agency, and sent Mother a cheque for £35. I also wrote to Col. Carey and General Atkinson asking for a reference for a job which I had applied for in India. I was on three months' notice and, with the continuing cutbacks in Iraq, I felt it was time to look for a more permanent job. I had applied for a five year appointment as 'Chief Inspector of Stores' in Simla, which would pay Rps. 2,250/month and for which I had been recommended by an engineer friend in Delhi.

Carey was sympathetic with my situation, and had written to the Director of Works and Buildings at the Air Ministry in London to try to secure a permanent Air Ministry contract for me in Iraq, saying that 'this Officer is without question the best Officer I have got'. He had asked permission to extend my contract as 'there is still considerable work to be done in Basra, and being some 400 miles from Baghdad, it is essential to have a thoroughly reliable Officer in charge'. However, he was extremely fair and also wrote to Pithkeathley, the Chief Controller of the Indian Stores Department in Simla, giving me a wonderful reference saying:

–   Mr H.C. Lott is an extremely conscientious and hard-working official with very high ideals and absolutely loyal;
–   He has a very wide general engineering experience covering bridge work, steel frame construction, reinforced concrete, water supply, ice plants, electrical supply and distribution and probably other things of which I do not know; but his general engineering knowledge is undoubtedly far above average, and he has also very good theoretical knowledge;
–   He has had control of a very large number of Indians and also of mixed parties of Indians, Arabs, and Persians, sometimes as many as 2 to 3 thousand (actually it was 8,000!)
–   I shall be extremely sorry to lose him if you decide to offer him the job, but at the same time I should be very glad to see him obtain an appointment which may be of a more settled character than anything I can offer him in this country.

In early December Air Marshall Sir John Salmond, head of RAF Iraq Command, came to Iraq and met with Carey in Baghdad before coming to Basra. I had a meeting with him after he had visited the camps and facilities in Basra and Amara, with which he was generally satisfied. After mentioning that all British troops would shortly be withdrawn, he asked the two Group Captains to leave the room and made a personal request to me to stay on for further service, thanking me for what I had done. Carey had obviously given me a good report and I later thanked him for his support.

Following Salmond's visit, I received and accepted an Air Ministry contract on the condition that it was on one month's notice, as I did not want to be prevented from taking up any good opportunity that might arise in the future. I had already received a direct invitation to China from Lt.Col. Butterworth RE to relieve a Canadian engineer who was going on long leave. It was attractive, well-paid, and would have given me an opening in a country destined for early development, but it was also very short-term, and local trouble was reported.

In December I used some of my spare cash to buy £200 worth of shares in each of Gokak Mills (an Indian textile company) and Barcelona Traction, estimating the total value of my assets, cash, and securities at the time as £3,650, with an income of £170 a year.

On Christmas Eve I went by small launch to Ashar Creek where I extracted two bellums and towed them to the RE Jetty. Mills, Morgan, and I then went in one, and the servants and grub in the other, for a picnic up Isolation Creek. We took photographs, collected reeds, and had a walk, before returning home and going for dinner to Lt.Col. and Mrs Smith's, where Dr Pfeil and Miss Hindleston were already present.

On Christmas morning I caught the train to Baghdad, not arriving until 8.15 pm on Boxing Day evening. In Baghdad I stayed in the White Lodge mess again with Col. Carey, J.W. Bardon, and L.D. Grand. Carey was away for a couple of days in Mosul, and when he arrived back he took me to see the new hospital at Hinaidi. We went on to the E&M mess for tea with Inglis, Edmonds and Johnson, but I felt unwell, shivering and vomiting, and was taken to the RAF hospital at North Gate where malaria was diagnosed again. After a couple of days in hospital and some heavy doses of quinine and aspirin, I recovered, and was able to join the others, and resume my duties on New Year's Day 1923.

My somewhat nomadic existence was evidenced by the four contact addresses in my diary:
c/o Cox & Co., 16 Charing Cross, London;
c/o Cox & Co., Hornby Road, Bombay;
c/o Royal Bank of Canada, Montreal;
c/o Imperial Bank of Persia, Basra.

Basra 1923

It was time to return to Basra, so Coles and I boarded the S.S. Zobaida on 2nd January for a six-day voyage down the Tigris. We disembarked at Amara where 'we spent two nights in Bertram's bungalow and dined at the 40th Pathans' (a Punjabi regiment) mess as the guest of Lt.Col. H.S. Tyndall, followed by the usual rubbers of bridge after dinner'.

Amara and its Silverware

After visiting the Amara cantonment with Coles, I called on Zaroun, a celebrated silversmith who was later commissioned to make articles for King Feisal. He was a member of the Sabaeans, followers of John the Baptist, a non-Muslim sect who were famous for their boat building and 'Amara' silverware. I asked Zaroun to make me two silver bon-bon dishes with Tigris river scenes etched on the flat rims. He used melted-down rupee coins for the silver, and he did the etching with a sharp steel point, filling it with a 'secret' material, probably antimony, which has survived years of cleaning. On an earlier visit in 1921 he had made me a beautiful silver cigarette case, for which I had paid him £6 and a bottle of whisky. The cigarette case had a perfect 'seal' where the two halves joined; it was admired in 1924 by a silversmith in Tokyo who would have given me almost anything to copy it. As a non-smoker, I found that the 6 cigarettes it held sufficed for the occasional offer of a cigarette to a guest.

From Amara we took the buoyage launch M247 downstream to Basra, stopping for a night at Kurnah, after a walk to the Kaimah Khan where we had refreshed ourselves with eau de vie and coffee. It was not long before I was back in Amara again; orders had been given to evacuate our troops there, and I had to arrange the dismantling programme. Whilst there, I discussed a compensation claim for Rps.97,700/- with a Mr Abdul Kasim-el-Khedery, and was invited to the wedding feast of a local Christian where the refreshments included champagne, whisky, fruit and cakes, and the entertainment was provided by 2 bands and some dancing girls. All the British residents and their wives were present, and I was introduced to the Mutasarrif.

Our Engineering Projects and a new Chief Engineer

In addition to my normal duties, I had been asked by Carey to design a reinforced concrete bridge; it took me many hours working late in the evenings to complete the detail. When I received orders from him to go to Baghdad for meetings, I had just written in my diary 'I am overwhelmed in the office'. Group Captain H. Cooper DSO travelled with me on the train, and 'we cooked our own breakfast in the lavatory – hot tinned fish, boiled eggs, hot buttered toast, tea and fruit'! In Baghdad we had meetings with the senior RAF Medical Officers, and visited the new hospital, the new power station (where the pole line was being strung), the MT garage, and the road across the aerodrome. At the E&M mess Carey demonstrated his skills at ping-pong and we played whisky poker after dinner.

In March 1923 Carey was replaced as Chief Engineer by Lt.Col. C.B.O. Symons CMG DSO, and I spent a week with him showing him all our projects in Basra, including the ice plant, filtration plant, pumping stations, and oil fired power station supplying both civilians and military forces, the workshops and brickfields, the new RAF hospital, Hyde Park Corner swimming pool, the RE central stores, sawmill, carpentry shop, the wireless station, the butchery incinerator, the IWT dockyard, and the new barracks and officers' quarters at No.7 Wharf, Maqil. We also had work upstream at Nahr Umar, which had been created as an anchorage to relieve the congestion at Maqil. The new RAF hospital at Makina was my biggest project – it had needed careful design, especially regarding its foundations, as the subsoil was estuarial mud into which it was possible to push a walking stick up to the hilt.

Morgan and I had to go to the old Combined hospital for an inoculation against the plague, and we invited the matron, Miss Oliver, Mrs Rutledge, Miss Edwards and Miss Clubb to dinner and bridge that evening. I survived the inoculation without much reaction, but Morgan spent three days in bed with a fever before being able to resume work. It was the end of the financial year and I was busy getting bills ready, inspecting accounts and stock-taking in the stores. I also had to attend tests of staff conducted by the Command Testing Board of which I was President.

Col. Carey came to Basra at the beginning of April, on his way back to England, and joined us for the Bachelors' Ball at the Makina Club. The next day we arranged a photograph, and gave him a farewell dinner on 7th April before he left for Bombay on the S.S. Varsova.

The staff officers in Basra at our farewell to Col. Carey (front centre)

A week later there was the Masonic Ball which Morris, Morgan and I attended after helping with the decorations; I invited Lt. S.J. & Mrs Stocks as my guests as they were soon to return to England. I 'sat out one dance with Miss Crozier' and left at 2.30 am, but the other two did not get back until 4.30 am. That night I only had 2½ hours sleep, as I still maintained my habit of getting up at 5 am in order to start work by 7 am.

Ur of the Chaldees and Babylonian tablets

It was during one visit to General Atkinson's headquarters at Nasiriyeh, close to Ur of the Chaldees, that I bought from an Arab eighteen Babylonian tablets covered with beautiful cuneiform inscriptions. Ur had been a great Sumerian city ages before the arrival of the Chaldeans, and had the reputation of being one of the most ancient centres of civilization in Mesopotamia. It was the location of a temple to the Moon God, Nanna, the patron deity of Ur, and was mentioned in the 11th chapter of Genesis as being the birthplace of Abraham.

I visited ancient Ur in March 1923, on an outing with the Masons, and we were lucky to be shown over the excavations by Mr (later Sir) Leonard Woolley who had recently uncovered the remains of the temple of the Moon God. He worked there for a total of 12 years, and was the leader of a joint expedition financed by the British Museum and the University Museum of Philadelphia. His lecture made all the difference to our visit; otherwise there was nothing to be seen but a lot of brick walls which had been repaired by many generations of Kings, who had nearly always put their names on the bricks. Unfortunately, our enjoyment was rather marred by a severe dust-storm that got up in the afternoon and obscured the sun. Our

Letter from Khammurabi, King of Babylon, to Sin-idinnam.

A Babylonian tablet

86

eyes, noses, and everything else were coated with the dust, our clothes became brown and we felt absolutely filthy.

Woolley said that the clay tablets which I had bought were inscribed and then baked about 4000 years ago, and that many thousands of them had been found.

Some years later I had them deciphered by the British Museum expert, Mr Gadd, who reported that they were all business documents dating from the Third Dynasty of Ur, about 2300 to 2100 BC. The documents included a lease of a house; timesheets of labourers with wages paid in grain (i.e. payrolls); stocks of corn and oil; a list of maid-servants (possibly slaves or concubines) and their masters; receipts for a quantity of barley and flour; and a record of some rings given as a present by the Governor of Umma to a certain Ur-Bau. A close examination of some of the tablets shows the 'signature', or mark of a rolled-on seal, beautiful intaglio, of the man for whom the document was written by the scribe. I gave away several of these 4000-year-old tablets as Christmas presents to old friends in Canada. I also lent two of them to a 96 year old aunt and was unable to find them after her death; so my very varied collection of records, dating from 200 years before Abraham, was reduced to the eight tablets which remain in the family today.

The date of the Flood, which is described not only in Genesis but also on Chaldean tablets, was about 700 years earlier, around 3000 BC. Now Woolley found a layer of clean clay at Ur, several feet thick, which had been deposited as a layer of silt during a catastrophic flood which had wiped out many cities and their inhabitants in the area. It was, however, a local disaster and confined to the lower Euphrates and Tigris, affecting an area of perhaps only 400 miles by 100 miles across. But for the inhabitants of that wide valley at that time it must have seemed as if it covered the whole world. Woolley found much painted pottery made by the people of Ur before the Flood, which was very different from the pottery of the people who populated the area later.

The Marsh Arabs and Shooting Trips in the Marshes

Our weekend shooting trips were generally for partridge on the banks of the Tigris between Basra and Amara, or for duck in the Marshes on the lower Euphrates. My memories of the Marshes are well described (below) by Wilfred Thesiger in his book entitled 'The Marsh Arabs' with whom he lived for much of the time between 1951 and 1957. His photographs, and those of mine thirty years previously, are almost identical.

The Marshes on the lower Euphrates

'Memories of that first visit to the Marshes have never left me: firelight on a half-turned face, the crying of geese, duck flying in to feed, a voice singing somewhere in the dark, canoes moving in procession down a waterway, the setting sun, crimson through the smoke of burning reed-beds, narrow waterways that wound still deeper into the Marshes. Stars reflected in dark water, the croaking of frogs, canoes coming home at evening, peace and continuity, the stillness of a world that never knew an engine.'

However, the Marsh Arabs, or Madan, had a bad name with the Arabs and English alike. In Arabic, 'madan' means dweller in the

Adan or Plain, and the nomads of the desert used it contemptuously to signify any of the Iraqi river tribes. Arabs can be snobs, and the more pretension of any tribe to pure Arab descent, the more its members despise the Marshmen for their dubious lineage. Even among the British in Iraq at the end of the First World War, the reputation of the Madan was bad, a legacy probably from when they had used the shelter of their Marshes from which to murder and loot both sides indiscriminately.

The British political officers had been too busy to concern themselves much with the Madan, and their visits generally only lasted a few days. When Europeans from Baghdad and Basra had gone to the Marshes for duck-shooting, they generally stayed with the richer sheikhs on the edge of the Marshes.

On one memorable trip in April 1923, I left Basra at 5 pm on a Saturday with Stocks and a friend of his, and we went up-river in a launch for a few hours, having dinner as we travelled. We had soup, then a minced beef shape (burger), followed by hot chicken and sausages (from a tin), and a pudding with tinned peaches. Having spent most of the previous night at a dance, I went to bed on the roof of the launch after dinner. We expected to reach our jumping-off point at midnight and intended to lay there, under the protection of a local Sheikh, until the next day.

At 1.30 pm I awoke with a gale of wind blowing and rain threatening so, rolling up my blankets, I descended into the launch to sleep the rest of the night there. In the morning we were told that we had stopped several miles short of our destination, owing to a leak under one of the shaft-bearing plates. It was not possible to do more than stop it up with wood and mud; running the engine was out of the question, so they had 'hove-to'. We then hailed a public launch coming down-river, carrying Arabs, chickens, and two sheep, and they came alongside and towed us back to Basra.

The following weekend young Stocks and I set off in a launch from Maqil and picked up a Sheikh, Abdul Sadar, who took us to an Arab village on the edge of the marshes where we tied up for the night. At 5 am the next morning, we took the launch into the marsh area towing two mashufs, long thin canoes used by the Madan for navigating through the reeds. All of us were armed with service rifles, and we shot over 20 wild boars before lunch, having approached them in the mashuf, or by wading through the marshes. It was generally useless to stalk them down-wind; they had good eyesight, but seemed hard of hearing if they were asleep.

In a mashuf in the Marshes on the lower Euphrates

Wild boars were the Marshman's natural enemy and often inflicted serious wounds on adults and children, so we did not feel any compunction in killing them, and the Madan certainly did not object.

We sometimes chased the boars through water eighteen inches deep, and, as we got closer, they could whip round and charge, approaching very fast through a smother of spray. One bullet was often not enough to stop an enraged boar, which would keep on coming and could do a lot of damage. Once we saw two big boars standing and watching us about a hundred yards away. We turned the canoe sideways and stood behind it. I fired and hit one of them; it immediately spun round, galloped off about twenty yards, then swerved and came straight at us, with the other close behind.

I fired again, but he never faltered; then again, and he still came on, and we only dropped the pair of them just before they reached the canoe.

The result of a wild boar shoot in the marshes

Social Life in Basra

A tennis party at the Makina Club in Basra

Socially the years in Basra were some of the most crowded of my life as I turned 40 in July 1923. That year, in my spare time, I played a lot of tennis, rather badly I fear despite much practice, because of the weakness of my wounded right arm. I played mostly with Morgan, Morris, Phillips, and Crawford, whom I beat occasionally, as they were not much better than me. We sometimes played up to five sets and had boys to pick up the balls and hand them to the server – each boy getting four pence for the evening.

A great deal of entertaining was possible for drinks were cheap, the best whisky costing only 4 shillings and 6 pence a bottle; wines and liqueurs were equally inexpensive. After tennis, or on my balcony, or at dinner, guests were frequent and numerous. My Indian servant Samuel, a Christian Madrasi, was a most capable butler, besides being an excellent cook on my tours of inspection.

In my Headquarters Mess in Basra, I had 17 British officers under my command. The number gradually became less as my economies and the reduction in our activities took effect. On the weekly guest night, we sometimes sat down as many as 40 at dinner. One of my guests was Lt.Col. John de Grey, a Knight of Grace of St John of Jerusalem, affiliated with the Masons. He was an epicure and a connoisseur of many things, but did not play bridge, and so, after dinner, we sat out upstairs with drinks on my verandah, talking until 11.30 pm.

The drink always flowed freely during the meal and after the Royal Toast which was always drunk in port. The general demand was for whisky sodas, and it was not unusual for a man to consume ten glasses on hot summer evenings, when the temperature was still well over 100 degrees. As we could not afford to have 400 bottles of soda water for our 40 guests, we invested in a soda-water making machine. During the evening, an Arab orderly operating this machine, would keep on filling the empty bottles and putting them back into the bath of ice, so that guests often had soda from the same bottle several times in an evening. In the great heat it was good to drink about two gallons of liquid every day.

My staff at RE House in Basra

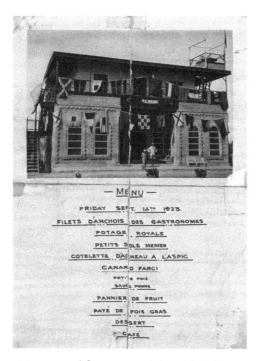

— MENU —

FRIDAY SEPT. 14TH 1923.

FILETS DANCHOIS DES GASTRONOMES

POTAGE ROYALE

PETITS SOLE MENIER

COTELETTE DAGNEAU A L'ASPIC

CANARD FARCI

PETITS POIS
SAUCE POMME

PANNIER DE FRUIT

PATÉ DE FOIS GRAS

DESSERT

CAFE

Menu card for guest night at RE House

Personally, being only a moderate drinker, I was always content with the gamut of wines and liqueurs served with the meal, but after dinner I drank only soda water, several bottles of it.

The menu cards for our guest nights in RE House were designed to be worth keeping as souvenirs and showed a photograph of the Mess with the menu neatly printed in black ink below. The example here shows RE House in Maqil bedecked in flags and my bed in the framework on the roof.

When the thermometer was over 100 degrees, Capt. Morgan and I would sometimes give a dinner party for the matron and sisters of the Military Hospital on a launch, which we were able to hire for Rps.5/6 per hour. We spread cushions on the roof and sped through the darkness to make a cooling breeze whilst we enjoyed cold drinks or dozing off on the return journey. The ladies really appreciated these outings as a chance to get away from their bungalows where the air was still and stifling.

A typical menu for the dinner, passed up from below through the trap door to the roof of the launch, was: olives, salmon mayonnaise, chicken and tongue with cold vegetables, fruit salad and cream, iced asparagus and claret cup for drink. Instead of finger bowls after the asparagus, a bowl of warm water with soap and a towel were passed up to us by Samuel.

Sometimes we would pick the ladies up later after dinner and just take a picnic on the launch to have whilst we lazed on the banks of the river at Gurnal Ali. One evening we took Misses Isabel Oliver, Rees-Jones, Leslie Graham and Madrell for a trip up-river to Coal Island and 'had claret cup, sandwiches, grapes and candies, and returned by midnight.' Occasionally we would invite them to a Ladies' night at the mess.

There was a cinema in Basra where a piano was played rather badly whilst we watched silent movies. The Amateur Dramatic Society, led by Mrs Stocks, put on plays at the Club, and there were concerts there too. On one occasion I entertained Morgan, Morris, and Col. Smith to the Eagle's Claw Show at the MT Theatre, before taking them on to the Club for supper.

A very gay week in early May started with a trip by launch to Ahwaz, a Persian town 100 miles up the Karun River. Morgan joined me and we hired a launch from the Government, taking it to the entrance of the Karun River, about 20 miles from Basra. We picked up a pilot at Muhammarah, just inside the Persian frontier, and travelled all night, reaching Ahwaz, or rather Bandar Nasiri, at 11 am. There we called on the British Vice Consul, and had a drink with him and two other Political Officers, before wandering the town and the bazaar; both were a little disappointing. In the river rapids just above the town I saw the first rock I had seen since returning from England 18 months earlier! We returned overnight and got back in time for work at 8 am on Monday morning. The meals that Samuel provided from the primus stove astonished Morgan who had never travelled with me before.

On the Wednesday night, I was one of three officers of the local garrison invited by the British Community of Basra, Baghdad, Muhammarah, and Bushire, to attend a farewell banquet at the Makina Club for Sir Percy and Lady Cox. It was a full-dress affair, with white tie and tailcoats, the third time I had worn mine in the last 18 months. About 100 guests of both sexes, including a few Arab notables, without their wives of course, sat down to a fine dinner which, after long speeches by Judge Woodman, Col. Ward and Sir Arnold Wilson, ended at midnight. I had a few words with Lady Cox who well remembered me when I was in Baghdad, and we laughed over incidents on the voyage out on the Dufferin in 1919.

On the following afternoon I accepted an invitation of the Indians of the Works Section in Maqil, to attend their reception to bid farewell to Lt. S.J. and Mrs Stocks, my officer and his wife, who were leaving for England. It was rather like a garden party, with a good brand of champagne being distributed amongst the senior guests. That same evening I had champagne again as the guest of the RE Mess Maqil at their dinner to bid the Stocks farewell.

Further Staff Reductions – Summer 1923

My main role during my two years in Basra was to reduce my establishment of officers and men to a small fraction of the initial numbers, in line with the Government's directive, whilst still carrying out all the projects which had been sanctioned. As the cutbacks took effect, I lost many officers who left for England, and those who remained had to put in more hours of work than would have been expected in any normal commercial enterprise. In this drive to cut costs I was greatly helped by the tremendous organising ability of my Personal Assistant, Morgan.

At the end of May I spent two weeks with Col. Symonds reviewing all our projects and agreeing the further staff cutbacks we would have to make. I met him at Amara where we visited the cemetery, the cantonment, the aerodrome, and LB powerhouse. Before returning to Basra, we visited Qalat Saleh and some brick kilns along the riverbank which were fed with reeds as fuel. A few months previously, I had distributed English pattern brick moulds to the Arabs to make samples, and told them that I would be calling for tenders for bricks soon. I was convinced that we could buy bricks cheaper than we could make them, even if the quality was not quite as good as ours. This turned out to be the case and, once I had established a reliable supply from local contractors, I was able to close our own brickfields and repatriate the Indians who were employed there. One of these Arab contractors was Mr Angoorly who owned the brickfields beside the river at Gurnal Ali.

Symonds told me that I had reduced my personnel more than Hinaidi had found possible, which I accepted as a compliment. Reductions was what I had been retained for, although every one of my officers kept telling me that the work could not be done well without the men that I told them to send away. It was true that I had to reduce the supervisory staff below the economic limit, but I had to cut my cloth according to my budget. When I arrived in Basra in January 1922 I had 2,950 Indians, and 500 Persians enrolled. In April 1923, this number was down to 1,070 Indians and, after I had made more cutbacks in June, there were only 700 enrolled Indians under my command.

In Basra I took Symonds to inspect the new hospital, the old and new offices, No.7 and No.11 Wharf buildings at Maqil, the brickfields, the CPH plants, the Makina sub-station, the facilities at Shaiba, and an area belonging to Abdul Ragab el Mirr. He was obviously satisfied with what he saw as, after his visit, I received a letter from him asking if I would stay until next March (1924).

Apart from work, I kept up my piano playing, was the organist at Masonic Lodge meetings, and often played the organ at Ashar church on Sunday evenings. When not entertaining or being entertained, I enjoyed quiet evenings in my room, reading, writing, or, more often, typing letters to friends and family. I noted that a letter I received from the Times Supply Agency in London had taken only 11 days to reach me in Basra – a record for me. In July 1923, the Nairn Transport Co. of Beirut had been awarded a contract to provide a weekly mail service from Haifa to Baghdad, so that mail could go by steamer from

England to Port Said, train to Haifa (16 hrs), and motor car from there to Baghdad (40 hrs), in a total of 8 or 9 days. This relieved the Air Force of the costly service it had been providing from Cairo to Baghdad.

The first small rainstorm which brought me down from my bed on the roof, was followed by a dust-storm and then a heavy thunderstorm. A bout of malaria with vomiting and fever at the end of the month interrupted my programme, but I was back at work after a couple of days. The hospital examined me and gave me something to take for dyspepsia. Morgan also spent a week in hospital with a fever in July.

As Sheikh Besa in my Arab costume

It was the King's birthday on 2nd June - an extremely hot day with the temperature up to 102 deg. I felt lazy, doing only a little work in the office in the morning. After a short game of tennis in the afternoon, I changed into my Arab Sheikh's costume and attended the Carnival in the evening as 'Sheikh Besa', remaining unrecognised until I revealed my identity, before returning home at midnight.

On 11th June the shamal started; a strong wind from the north which brought with it dust storms, sometimes obliterating the sun; at least it was better than the hot and humid south wind. The following morning we packed up our belongings and moved everything in two barges from Ashar Creek to our next home, the RE House at No.7 Wharf, Maqil. It was a strenuous day with a sandwich lunch on the balcony and much to be done to make the house really habitable. There were five officers in the mess with me, Morgan, Morris, Inglis, White and Phillips. The building had been used by the Inland Water Transport, and their look-out platform above the roof was large enough to provide me with a sleeping place for most of the year. Rain was very unusual, and only on stormy nights did I have to pick up my bed, and descend to the roof and down to my bedroom below, to sleep under cover. One great advantage of my eyrie was that the mosquitoes never seemed to worry me there, whereas all my officers had to sleep under mosquito nets which surrounded the bed and blocked the cooling breeze of the overhead fan.

The highest temperature at Ashar in June 1923 was 119 deg. and the average maximum during the month was 105.5 deg., with an average minimum of 80 deg. To relieve the heat on several evenings during June and July, Morgan and I took the ladies, most frequently Miss Oliver, Miss Madrell and Miss Leslie Graham, out for a spin in the Vauxhall, or on launch trips up-river. One evening there was an informal out-of-doors dance at the Civil Sisters, near Basra City.

Guest nights on Fridays were an opportunity to maintain contact and enhance relationships with senior personnel in the Basra community. On 6th July I invited Colonel S.C. Ward CE DSO MBE to his first evening with the RE Services, together with Wing Commanders Tyrell and Glymer from the RAF Combined hospital, and three other RAF doctors, plus Chapman and Challoner. On other occasions I entertained May from APOC, Murray from Customs, Nodwell from RAF Medical Services, White from 1st Sappers & Miners, Langdon, and Beveridge from the RAMC, and Mr & Mrs Garbett.

The Sunday before my 40th birthday, I took Morgan and Inglis to dine at Luna Park, and we went on to Basra for a drive and a walk before returning home. The dinner, with two bottles of wine and four short drinks at Rp.1/- each, cost a total of Rps.37/8.

Feisal appointed King of Iraq

Three years after the British victory in 1918 over the Turks and the Germans, Emir Feisal, third son of King Sharif Hussein of the Hedjaz, was chosen as King of Iraq in March 1921 at the Cairo Conference attended by Winston Churchill, Sir Percy Cox, Gertrude Bell, Arnold Wilson, and Colonel T E Lawrence amongst others. The decision had been assisted by Lawrence who had lobbied Churchill before he left London and by Gertrude Bell who had done the same with Sir Percy Cox in Baghdad. Feisal had been accompanied by Lawrence during the 'Revolt in the Desert' and with his sacks of gold he had probably contributed more to the successful advance towards Damascus than Lawrence himself.

Gertrude Bell felt sure that there was only one workable solution to the problem of who to appoint as the King of Iraq: "a son of Sharif Hussein and for choice Feisal." Sharif Hussein was a descendant of the prophet Muhammad and guardian of Mecca. Yet among the Iraqis there was not much sympathy for his assertion that he spoke for all the Arabs. They were Mesopotamian; he was from Mecca. They felt that he represented Britain; they wanted someone who represented them. Nevertheless, now that the French had thrown Feisal out of Damascus he was, in Gertrude's opinion, very much the first choice. His military experience in the Arab Revolt against the Turks, his administration of Syria, his diplomatic skills, his depth of character and his charisma would make him the perfect leader.

However, as a Sunni ruler in a country with a Shiite majority, Feisal would have to base his legitimacy on his Sharifian roots, and most importantly on his descent from Muhammad. He had never before set foot in Iraq; he knew little of the people he would rule, of the land over which he would reign, or of the history he would inherit. He had no knowledge of the Iraqi tribes, no friendships with their sheikhs, no familiarity with the terrain - the marshes in the south, the mountains in the north, the grain fields, and the river life - and no sense of connection with its ancient past.

He even spoke a different dialect of Arabic, a mixture of Hedjaz, Egyptian, Syrian, and Turkish. Yet Gertrude knew he had the intelligence to learn quickly and the charisma to lead effectively. He sent for her frequently to ask her advice and she did her utmost to assist him in his new role.

'In British Occupation', the words appearing for a few years as an overprint and surcharge on Iraq stamps, officially ended when King Feisal took over and started the process of forming an Arab government in Iraq.

During the nine years of his reign Feisal did a great deal to unify the many tribes of his country and gave them strong leadership. Unfortunately, the kingdom did not last many years for, after the assassination of his grandson, King Feisal II, the country became a Republic as it is today.

Soon after Feisal's arrival in Baghdad in July 1921, Gertrude had helped to arrange dinners to bring the King together with the influential leaders of the city. Dinners had been held by Sir Percy and Lady Cox for Feisal, and then by Feisal for the sheikhs of the Tigris and the Euphrates. I was to attend similar dinners when Feisal visited Basra in June 1923.

My Dinners with King Feisal – June 1923

On 22nd June1923 the King paid his first official visit to his Southern Province, the Basra Liwa, arriving by river and staying in the house of the Arab Governor, His Excellency Ahmed Pasha Sanna, the Mutasarrif. There were great decorations and illuminations, and I watched his arrival at Ashar.

Having been ordered by H. M. the King.
The First Chamberlain

requests the pleasure of

Col. Lott's

company at a dinner to be given at the residence of
the *Mutasarrif of Basrah Liwa*
on *Monday the 25th June, 1923, at 8 p m.*

R. S. V. P.

His Excellency Ahmed Pasha Sanna, the Mutasarrif, Basra Liwa

Suq-el-Dijaj Quarter,
Basrah City, 24th June, 1923.

Sheikh Ahmed Nouri Eff: Bashayan,
Rais-el-Baladiyah, on behalf of the Basrah
Municipality requests the pleasure of
Lt. Col. Lott's D.D. R.E. services
margil
company to Dinner to be given to-night at
8.0 p.m., *at* his residence *in* "Suq al Dijaj"
in Honour of H.M. The King.

As Deputy Director of RE Services, I was invited to a dinner at 8.00 pm on Saturday 23rd June, given by the Mutasarrif at his residence in Pasha Street, in honour of His Majesty the King. Besides the Senior British Resident in Basra and myself, probably the largest employer of Arab labour, there were few other Britishers in the company of about sixty. The King sat directly opposite his host across a narrow table. On the King's right was his (Arab) Minister of Justice and on his left the Senior British Resident. I sat on the right of our host, the Mutasarrif, and so directly opposite the other Britisher.

Feisal spoke to us foreigners in French - he had become accustomed to using French during his time in Syria and probably felt more comfortable with it than English. My diary does not describe the meal, but I noticed that the King was drinking Perrier water imported from France, whilst the rest of us were offered sour milk or locally made soda water. Alcohol was, of course, not served as Mohammedans do not drink alcohol, at least not in public.

On the following evening, I was guest of Sheikh Ahmed Nouri Eff Bashayan, the Rais-el-Baladiyah or 'Lord Mayor' of Basra, at a dinner at his residence, Suq al Dijaj, in honour of the King. The meal of about 12 courses was excellently served and I sat next to Hashim Beg, His Excellency the Naquib, a millionaire landowner and chief religious figure of the Sunni community, with whom I was able to converse a little in French.

On the third night, Monday 25th June, I was a guest of the King who gave a return banquet for about 80 people on the roof of the Mutasarrif's house. Dinners in the heat of summer were a real trial; the nights were hardly any cooler than the days, and sweat poured off our brows as we ate our way through heaped platters of eggplant, stuffed vine leaves, roast lamb, rice, and fresh fruit, and listened to formal speeches.

This particular meal was worse than a nightmare for me as I watched the old roof, with its many layers of mud-cum-cowdung to make it water-tight, supported on long spans of palm-tree timbers, move alarmingly up and down. I felt sure that it had not been designed to carry a load of eight tons or more, with waiters scurrying to and fro, and I realised all too well that if the roof gave way, we would be taken down through the lower floors and reach ground level buried, King and all, in a mass of earth and timbers.

I could only speak a few words of Arabic, and did not know enough about the resilience of old palm trees to mention my concerns. In any event it would have been impossible to warn the King and his guests that the dinner should be cancelled, so I suffered in silence.

A few days after the King had left Basra, the Agent of Hashim Beg called and said "His Excellency was delighted to make your acquaintance the other evening. Would you do him the honour of having a meal with him? If so, what meal and when?"

Realising that I could not refuse, and not wanting to face another Arab dinner, I replied, "Thank His Excellency very much for his kind invitation. I should be very pleased to have breakfast with him next Wednesday morning at 8 o'clock."

Now Hashim Beg had three palaces in Basra for his wives. During the War, the Army had commandeered two of them - the palaces, not the wives - and as the Senior Claims Officer on the Compensation Committee in Basra, I was aware that the question of compensation had still to be settled.

The old chap must have wondered what Englishmen had for breakfast; in any case, being a Muslim, he could not serve bacon. So, we had the following separate courses, which, out of politeness, I had to eat with appreciation, not knowing what else was to follow. The meal started with soup, followed by fish, eggs, lamb cutlets, boiled chicken, cheese, toast and preserves, and tea. Then came fresh fruit, coffee, and cigarettes, and finally, a bowl of water in which to dip our fingers, although knives, forks and spoons had been provided. No wonder it is an Arab custom to express one's appreciation of a meal by belching!

King Feisal stands out as the tallest in the party at Zobeir

On the third day of his State visit Feisal went to see the ancient walled city of Zobeir, just south of Basra, with an entourage of armoured cars, aeroplanes, camels, and horses. I had an invitation and took Carson and Miss Lorraine to see the welcome he received. He left his car when he saw some Arab horsemen galloping from the town to greet him. I noticed his annoyance when he was smothered in dust kicked up by the horses and he returned to his car.

H.M. KING FEISAL OF IRAK *from a portrait by* AUGUSTUS JOHN

King Feisal

King Feisal's visit to Zobeir – June 1923

Working with the RAF

Inspection Flights

In August 1923 I received orders from GHQ in Baghdad to go, once a month, to Nasiriyeh on the Euphrates. I was to inspect and give advice to the British officers commanding the 1st Arab Levy Battalion on the defences of the town and the RB aerodrome which they were constructing, against possible, almost probable, raids by the neighbouring Saudis.

De Havilland DH 9A

My first journey was by a two-seater RAF de Havilland DH 9A from the RAF aerodrome at Shaiba, 17 miles from my HQ. I left Maqil by moonlight in the Ford at 3.45 am and found the plane ready when I arrived at the aerodrome. It was my first flight since a test flight in a twin-engine Handley Page machine in France in 1919. Nasiriyeh is about 90 miles from Shaiba and the flight took 1 hour and 5 minutes, with Flt.Lt. Saunders DFC MM as the pilot.

De Havilland DH 9A

In Nasiriyeh I met Lt.Col. Archer of the 1st Iraq Levy Battalion, and other officers, including Col. Dent on inspection duty. After an inspection tour around the Levy Camps, a nap after lunch, and half an hour's attempt to start the engine, we left Nasiriyeh aerodrome at 5.45 pm, and I arrived back at the mess at 7.45 pm, after sunset. That evening after dinner I wrote up my report and did not turn in until 11.15 pm; it had been a long day.

On my second visit to Nasiriyeh to inspect the defences, I went by train, but owing to the infrequency of the trains from Basra, and a bad connection at Ur Junction, the inspection cost me three whole days and two nights absence from my job, so I decided to make a landing strip close to our Maqil HQ and go by plane in future. The plane used to taxi to my car and pick me up at 6 am, dropping me in time for breakfast with the officers of the Arab Levies at Nasiriyeh. As the Basra Times reported in September 1923: "The aeroplane as a time-saver is coming into its own. The other day Colonel Lott, Deputy Director of Works, RE Services, travelling by air, made an early start for Nasiriyeh, completed a four-hour inspection and returned in time for luncheon in Basra."

Apart from flights to and from Nasiriyeh, I was flown by the RAF to Amara, 140 miles from Basra. Flying was not without its risks and there was always the hazard of a sudden dust storm producing complete invisibility. In the two-seater plane, which the pilot loaded with sand-bags when he was flying alone, the cock-pit was open and very draughty, making air-sickness which I suffered from in the often bumpy conditions, a most embarrassing experience. It had not occurred to me to use a paper bag, as I was offered some years later, when I was flown in a chartered Moth plane in Kenya and Tanganyika in 1930.

The RAF rescuing a stranded motor vehicle in the desert

I received a letter in September from Col. Carey, informing me that General Stuart at the Air Ministry had mentioned my name, having heard that I was 'an excellent administration officer for a headquarters office'. The General thought it likely that money would be voted for an augmentation of the Air Force, which would mean increased expenditure and certain demands for staff for the preparation and execution of schemes. Carey wondered if I might be interested in calling at the Air Ministry if I decided to stay in England when I returned home.

Working with Air Marshall Sir John Salmond

In January 1924, as controller and adviser on all capital expenditure from the RE budget in Basra, I accompanied Air Marshall Sir John Salmond, the Commander-in-Chief, on his inspection of all RAF establishments in the area.

Of all the very high ranking officers and Army commanders, including the C-in-C in France, and their Chief Engineers whom I had met in the 9 years of my Army experience, John Salmond was outstanding in intellect, personality, and leadership.

AIR MARSHAL ENGAGED.—The engagement is announced of Air Marshal Sir John Salmond and the Hon. Monica Grenfell, elder daughter of Lord Desborough. 1924

AIR-MARSHALL SIR JOHN SALMOND

Socially, too, he was most excellent company, as I found when we were fellow guests in one or other of the RAF Officers' messes, during his visits. No-one could have been more thorough or knowledgeable in his inspections of the units under his command.

During his inspection of the Armoured Car Company in Basra, I was present when he asked the sergeant in charge of the Company's armoury for a rifle to be taken out of one of the racks. His first remark upon opening it and looking through the barrel was "Is that dust or dirt?", "Show me another". After looking through the second rifle, he said "It's more like dirt than dust". He asked to see a third and then said in a damning tone, "And I'm sure it is dirt". Not many Commanders-in-Chief would have been so meticulous and taught such a lesson to an inefficient unit.

The same day he inspected an RAF Stores unit and I saw him take a small article from a rack of spare parts and ask for the tally card. The number of articles shown on the tally did not agree with the articles which he had counted in the rack. So he tried another article with the same result, showing in both random instances that the store-keeping records of the Company were unreliable, and therefore rotten.

Before returning to Baghdad, Sir John Salmond made a point of thanking me for having acceded to his request of exactly a year before, to stay on an extra 12 months to continue my work of reducing the staff and men under my administration, before retiring from the Forces and leaving the country to resume my civilian career.

Managing my Arab Workforce

The Arabs I employed locally were recruited by agents, each bringing a gang of 25 and acting as foreman of the gang. Of course the agents extracted a part of the pay of each man for themselves. So instead of the usual practice of the ganger being paid a lump sum, I arranged a reform of the pay system so that every member of the gang individually received his one rupee pay for each day he worked for me. How much of that he had to pay to the agent was not my concern; at least he saw the money that he earned. It added to the work of my Pay Officer, but it was a reform that was necessary.

If I found the men idling on my rounds of inspection, I blamed and punished the ganger in the presence of the men, for he generally did nothing but sit and watch them. As I could not fine him, I threatened him with corporal punishment. In this way I got much more work done, especially as I was able to select my gangers, discriminating between the good and bad ones, as my need of Arabs diminished.

I asked a British officer of the Arab Levies why the men or the ganger did not turn on me and retaliate, especially when I was alone. He said that, as long as he felt that there was any justice in the punishment, an Arab would take it. However, any kind of corporal punishment was later banned, and, in any case, it could not have been used with Indians, whether Punjabis, Sikhs or Hindus; a white man was considered by them to be of a lower caste.

My Personal Assistant, Morgan, had an excellent and novel way of punishing his Arab servant, having warned him that he would be fined 5 rupees if he did a certain thing. When pay-day came, Morgan abstracted a 5 rupee note and set fire to it with a match in front of the offending servant. So the man was fined, but could not accuse his master of enriching himself by withholding the money. Mentioning Morgan and his efficiency in organising, he used to go into an office and find out what each Indian clerk had done the day before - all entries being dated. Thus, he quickly found out how many men in that office could be dispensed with and repatriated to India. At this time I was repatriating about 100 Indians a week.

My success, so largely due to Morgan's help, in reducing the cost to the British Exchequer of my establishment, was really responsible for Sir John Salmond asking me, in January 1923, to stay for another 12 months, although my rank was then a grade higher than was warranted by the job.

Perhaps it was my reputation for early rising, hard work, and efficiency, which gave rise to my nick-name, 'Lottsky', which was referred to in the tribute paid to me in an article in The Times of Mesopotamia on 1st March 1924 when I finally left Iraq and was demobilised.

My life-long habit of early rising enabled me to go round outside jobs to see if the work had been properly organised so that the hundreds of men were able to start on time. This prompted one of my Basra officers to remind me of a verse in the Bible in Proverbs, chapter 27, verse 14:

"He that blesseth his brother with a loud voice rising early in the morning, it shall be counted a curse unto him."

Managing my Indian Workforce

Besides being Senior Claims Officer in Basra, I had to preside at the local Claims Committee hearings at Amara. My diary records that one claim was for compensation to the Arab owners of 15,000 date palms in a garden which they had lost during the military occupation. Damage to buildings, which had been commandeered and then returned to the owners, had also to be assessed and paid for, including two of the three palaces owned by Hashim Beg.

At about this time, 25 years before India was eventually granted Independence, I became aware that my Sikhs, working as brick-makers, electricians, wiremen and linesmen, carpenters, and pattern-makers, were being infected with the agitation in India for 'Swaraj', as Independence from British rule was called. To demonstrate their point, they wore black 'puggarees' (turbans) and long 'kirpans' (swords).

JANUARY 12, 1924

NEW YEAR'S HONOURS.

Sardar Sahib Indar Singh.

His Excellency the Viceroy of India has been pleased to confer the title of, Sardar Sahib on Mr. Indar Singh Superintendent in the office of the Senior Works officer at Basrah. He has received a congratulatory message from H. E. the High Commissioner of 'Iraq.

Sardar Sahib Indar Singh (late recently Deputy Director of R. E. Services at Basrah) came to this country in February 1916 and by his indefatigable labour, whether in carrying out the onerous duties of office work tactfully or during the late war, in recruiting men for the Forces, has done the State some service (writes a correspondent.)

That his eight years of careful service have been appreciated by his immediate superior officer (Colonel H. C. Lott, M.C.,) is both sufficient token of the solicitude of the Colonel for the welfare of his men and an honour to the Staff. It has ....

113

As I naturally objected to a wireman attending to a fuse in my office or quarters wearing a sword, I tackled my Office Superintendent, Mr Indar Singh. He was a tall, impressive man, whose full beard belied his real age, which may have been under 30. I told him that in so demonstrating for Swaraj, they were being disloyal to the King of England, who was their ultimate employer and the source of their pay and livelihood.

Now I had provided the sect with buildings for their places of worship, or 'gurdwaras', and I was sure that in these gurdwaras, which were not open to non-Sikhs, sedition was being preached. I asked him about the kirpans, a sword or small dagger, which all Sikhs are bound to wear, and he produced his, a miniature one, from his waistcoat pocket, demonstrating that long kirpans were not necessary.

He then said, "In one month, Sahib, you will see no black pugarrees and no long kirpans." And so it was, except for one obstinate Sikh whom I naturally selected as one of the next batch of Indians to be repatriated as redundant in the economy measures!

So, hopefully, I put Indar Singh's name forward to Baghdad for inclusion in the recommendations for honours in the Viceroy of India's 1924 New Year's Honours List. To my very great surprise and delight, and Indar Singh's intense pleasure and pride, he received the courtesy title of 'Sirdah Sahib', which in India would be considered like a knighthood. Perhaps my good luck in the year that followed, was, in part, due to the blessings and prayers of Sirdah Sahib Indar Singh. He kept in touch after I left and wrote to me in London in 1927.

In Basra I had, besides Muslims and Sikhs, a few Hindus working for me, and there was a Hindu Regiment in the Basra garrison. If a Hindu died, he was cremated in a small plot of ground which I had reserved for them. There was an official ration of so many pounds of wood for such an eventuality, and wood was scarce in Iraq, as well as a ration of some pounds of 'ghee' (clarified butter).

Apparently the ration was found to be too small and I was therefore asked to increase the quantities for the next pyre! As I was never present at any open-air cremation I never really knew if the request for more fuel was justified, or whether the extra was used for other purposes.

My introduction to the local Arabs of the method of making English-pattern bricks, was one of the factors which contributed to my success in replacing enrolled Indian craftsmen with Arabs. They had responded well to my tenders for the millions of our type of bricks required for the new Makina Military Hospital, my principal building job. The old Arab bricks were little different from those made in Mesopotamia over 3,000 years earlier, some centuries before Nebuchadnezzar had started to advertise himself and his authority on the bricks made in his reign.

As well as producing bricks, we made building plaster or 'plaster of Paris' from locally quarried gypsum, making full use of local resources, just as we had done by using the experimental oil wells at Quaiyarah for making paraffin for our engines in Mosul.

Autumn 1923

There had been an outbreak of cholera in Basra during the summer, and one or two deaths, so my arrangements to leave for Amara in August were cancelled by the Senior Medical authorities, as I and my launch crew had not yet been fully protected by a second inoculation.

There were no Muslims working on 23rd August as we watched the annual procession commemorating the murder of Iman Hussein ibn Ali, the grandson of the prophet Muhammad. The sacrificial 'victim' (not dead) was carried on a bier, with his head much lower than his body, and thus out of sight. A raw calf's neck – with flies on it – took the place of the man's head. His feet stuck out and his hands also, but two daggers were visible, 'thrust' into his chest, giving every appearance of a decapitated man. I believe that when the British first occupied Iraq they had prohibited a real sacrifice.

The procession commemorating the murder of Imam Hussein ibn Ali

That month I received another inspection visit from Col. Symons, who stayed for a week, during which I took over responsibility for the construction of the Peace Cemeteries at Makina and Amara from the Deputy Director of the Imperial War Graves Commission. We cut out the proposed irrigation scheme to reduce cost, and decided on the location for the Mohammedan monument. I also took Col. Symons and Col. Durham down-river to see a possible site for the Memorial to the Missing.

We were reducing our presence in Amara, and I went there for three days in early September, with Capt. Peake and Calcutt, an auctioneer, travelling by launch overnight and arriving late the following afternoon, having missed the 2.30 pm opening of the bridge at Amara. We were met there by Lt.Col. Tyndall and dined with the 40th Pathans, staying in the E&M bungalow as usual. The next day I showed Calcutt around the cantonment and buildings, and spent a couple of hours in the Mutasarrif's office discussing rent issues, leaving by launch at 1.30 am on the Wednesday morning for the 14 hour trip back down-river.

A.S. Roden had gone to Amara to help Calcutt prepare for the auction of the facilities, and I flew up and spent a busy day with both of them before the sale started on 8th October. The sale of 136 buildings and huts raised Rps.72,000/-, equal to £5,000 at Rps.14.3 to £1; the lowest rate of the year to date. The sale of the surplus stores took place the following morning and was completed by 1 pm, so that I was free to join Nugent, Watkins, and Aston on a shooting party across the river at 2.30 pm. We took 2 Ford cars, 1 beater, and 5 dogs, and came back with 6½ brace.

I spent the next morning in the office issuing instructions for the closure of Amara and discussed the future of the wireless station with Capt. Nugent. Back in our RE House in Maqil on Friday afternoon, I had tiffin, a bath and change, and then went to the Ashar bazaar to do some shopping, visiting the new Hospital on the way. I had to go back to Amara in December with Bardon and Roden to call on the Administration Inspector, C.C. Ashton, and receive the claims made by landowners for damage done to their properties during the War and the Army's occupation. As President of the Claims Committee, I spent the next two days settling claims, before taking the launch back down-river on the Friday. We just got through the Amara bridge before it closed and reached the Majar Kabir Regulator at about 8.00 pm, tying up against the garden of the Irrigation Bungalow. In the morning we walked over to the Abu Sidra area for some shooting and got 15 birds, but lost a dog in the process, and had to go back up-stream for 2¼ hours to find it.

Flt.Lt. Saunders was my pilot for my September visit to Nasiriyeh. We flew at 2,000-3,000 ft and I had 3½ hours there with Col. Archer and Capt. Clarke before returning in time for lunch. The last half hour of the return trip was bumpy, and I was very air sick. Four months later, on a similar flight to Nasiriyeh, Saunders crashed the plane and was killed, together with his air mechanic.

A trip to Baghdad and back on the train, to meet with Col. Symons, Lt.Col. Henderson and Mr Harvey of the Exchequer and

Audit Department, took six days in mid-November. My companion in the new compartment on the way up was Mr J.C. Mackie of Younger & Co, brewers of Edinburgh; he was good company, and we were able to read and relax on the journey. In Baghdad with Col. Symons and his team, I went through my estimate and work plans for 1924 on which I had been working for much of the previous two weeks. He took me to Hinaidi again where we met Lt.Col. W.S. Blunt and inspected the new hospital. Whilst in Baghdad I also spent a couple of afternoons in the bazaar, buying Persian prints (a large bedspread Rps.10/- and a pair of door curtains Rps.10/-) and two engraved brass bowls. I noted in my diary that on the return train journey 'a Patriarch of the Assyrians was the TTI – the travelling ticket inspector'!

The new hospital in Basra was nearing completion and took up a lot of my time inspecting all the facilities before we handed them over to the RAF on 30th November. I had to raise Cain about the lack of speed in chasing up the final snagging jobs. We had had strong winds and torrential rains which had created a lot of mud on the site, but it did enable us to check that the drainage system was working properly. After hand-over, the only complaint we had from Wing Commander Glynn related to the operating and X-ray theatres.

The old hospital was evacuated; it was not safe, and we arranged for the disposal of the buildings and materials. We also demolished the old RE House and other facilities which had become surplus to requirements. In the last few months our numbers had continued to reduce and at our guest nights we drank toasts to the officers who were leaving for England.

During the autumn we arranged evening outings with the sisters from the hospital, and Morgan spent a lot of time with Miss Leslie Graham, 'his present fancy', taking her for all-day trips on the launch. She, Miss Madrell, Miss (Dr) Enid Pfiel, Miss Clubb, and Miss Oliver were our most regular guests. There was tennis as usual in the afternoons, sometimes with the ladies, and bridge after dinner most evenings at which I won or lost a few rupees.

November was the month for writing and sending my Christmas cards and letters, but this year I was also starting to apply for jobs, and I cabled Trollope & Colls in Shanghai in answer to an advertisement in the Times.

Over the Christmas period we went to see a Revue at the RAF Stores Depot by Francis Gerrard entitled 'A Night Out'; there was a Fancy Dress Ball on New Year's Eve for which I dressed once again as a Bedouin Sheikh, and I took a few of my officers to a Boxing Tournament at the MT Theatre in Makina.

The General Election in England in December had been inconclusive, and in January 1924 Ramsay MacDonald led a minority Labour Government, supported by H.H. Asquith's Liberals. The pound dropped from Rps.1410 to 1440, and there was speculation regarding the future of the garrison in Mespot.

It was getting much colder and we lit a fire in the mess most evenings now. On the coldest morning of the winter the mercury dropped below 40 degrees on my balcony, and for the first time I had an oil stove in my quarters. At the end of January exceptionally heavy rains caused flooding and the cantonment became very muddy. Storms caused a breakdown in the Basra electricity supply one night, and trains from Baghdad were held up by floods on the line. This was followed by a deluge in February which put Makina entirely under water.

My Last Shooting Trips

Capt. Inglis and I enjoyed a quiet weekend in early December, taking a launch up-river one Saturday evening, and spending Sunday 'walking about with guns, fishing at El Shafi and lazing'. He was my preferred companion on these trips - he was sadly killed in an RAF plane crash a few years later. We had no luck with the guns as the birds were too high and too few, but we returned to No.7 Wharf refreshed in time for breakfast on the Monday morning.

On Christmas Eve Inglis and Gingold joined me on a Government launch for a longer partridge shoot. We reached Ezra's Tomb after 9½ hours, just after midnight. I slept on the roof of the launch and found, on awaking, the deck and my pillow covered with a heavy white frost. Scraping some frost off with a spoon, I applied it to the faces and necks of my companions sleeping below! Such a low temperature in Iraq was unusual; the following day was not so cold, with a maximum of 76 degrees and a minimum of 42 degrees at night.

With Capt. Inglis on a shooting trip

We cast off next morning at 6.30 am and went further upstream through the Narrows, shooting 35 black partridges before we tied up to have our Christmas dinner and spend the night at Qalat Saleh village. Our dinner was excellent and consisted of soup, beef cutlets, roast partridge with cauliflower and potatoes followed by plum pudding.

During the next two days, between Qalat Saleh, Abu Sidra and Majar Kabir, we bagged about 30 black partridge each day, as well as one or two hares, making our total for the weekend 115 partridge and 6 hares. On the way back we stopped for a walk through the bazaar at Qalat Saleh, before tying up for the night at

Ezra's Tomb. An Arab offered to take us duck-shooting the next morning, but we had to refuse as we had run out of cartridges.

When we got back to Basra I delivered partridges to Matron & Sisters (12), Officers at RAF Stores (8), S.A. Smith, J.J. O'Connor and A.S. Roden (6), Dr Enid Pfeil (2), Morris and the Garbetts (3).

Rain and a soft south wind rather spoiled the sport on a weekend trip up the Euphrates with Robert Angoorly in January. We sat in the butts amongst the reeds, waiting for the evening flight of duck and geese, and then waded back through the water to our canoe, and thence to the launch for the night. We went out again on Monday at 5.00 am for the morning flight, before starting back to the RE House at 7.45 am, having breakfast on the launch on the way.

My final shooting trip, just before I left in February, was again with Inglis. We spent four nights on the launch, calling in at the reed village of Gurnal Ali to pick up Abdu Sadar, before going to the IWT dockyard where we attached ourselves alongside the ship HC 1, a paddle hospital carrier. It towed us through the night to Ezra's Tomb, from where we went under our own steam to shoot in the area around Qalat Saleh village. Our bag for the four days was 208 birds, all partridges except for one quail, despite a comment in my diary that 'the area had been denuded by Amara sportsmen'!

Farewell to Iraq in 1924

On 15th January I attended a dinner for Air Marshall Sir John Salmond at Group Headquarters. He had flown in to Shaiba for an inspection the following day which I attended; it lasted from 9.00 am until 5.15 pm with only a break for an hour or so at the new hospital, where we were entertained to lunch. The inspection included the central powerhouse, the IWT and RAF stores depot, the new hospital, rest camp, RAF prison, Group HQ offices, and barracks. The next day he carried out a detailed inspection of

No.3 Armoured Car Company, after which he called me to one side and said goodbye, adding "Thank you very much for all the hard work you have done", and expressing his pleasure that I had stayed on for the year after his last visit.

I spent most of the last two weeks of January and first two weeks of February writing many letters, tidying up my papers, and carrying out final inspections before handing over my responsibilities. In January I had received an offer from Khan Bahadur Mirza Muhammad to buy my 25 shares in the Times Printing & Publishing Co. Ltd. for Rps.2,400/-; they had cost me Rps.2,100/- when I bought them in November, and I decided to take the quick profit. I also sold my piano for Rps.1,200/- and remitted £300 back to London that month.

Lt.Col. H.W. Henderson arrived on 9th February from Baghdad to take over from me. Over the next 10 days I showed him round the works we had in progress and all the plants & facilities we were managing, formally handing over my duties as Senior Works Officer to him on Friday 22nd February. The week of the 18th-22nd February involved a continual series of farewells and dinners.

On the Tuesday there was a dinner at Group Headquarters, hosted by Group Captain Ivan Courtney CBE and Squadron Leader R.E. Saul DFC, to say farewell to the Officers of the 5/7 Rajputs and myself. On Wednesday I handed over my duties as Organist at the Installation Banquet of the Masons in the Basra Club, where Morgan and I were toasted as 'Departing Brethren'; I replied and finished with a musical sketch.

On Thursday I attended a reception given for me as a farewell party by my senior Indian staff, headed by my Office Superintendent with his new title of Sirdar Sahib Indar Singh. The tennis court was beautifully decorated with bunting and electric lights, and the approach to the court had three triumphal illuminated arches. Refreshments were served and the band of the

5/7 Rajput Regiment played 'choice selections of music' for the occasion. In his toast to me Sirdar Sahib Indar Singh said:

"We are gathered here to bid bon voyage to our popular Chief, Colonel H.C. Lott MC. During the past two years of Colonel Lott's term of office we have all been very contented, and we are all very sorry to lose such a kind, courteous, but firm Commanding Officer. To each one of us Colonel Lott has left a legacy; an example in character building, industry, and efficiency, and steady, honest work."

The Menu for my Farewell Dinner at the Makina Club

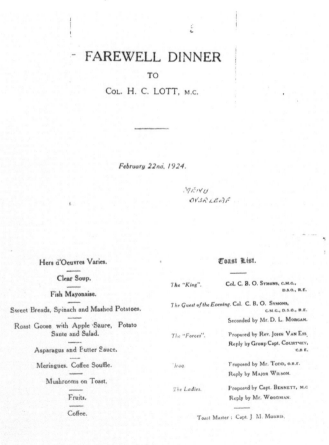

FAREWELL DINNER

TO

COL. H. C. LOTT, M.C.

February 22nd, 1924.

MENU
OVERLEAF

Hors d'Oeuvres Varies.

Clear Soup.

Fish Mayonaise.

Sweet Breads, Spinach and Mashed Potatoes.

Roast Goose with Apple Sauce, Potato Saute and Salad.

Asparagus and Butter Sauce.

Meringues. Coffee Souffle.

Mushrooms on Toast.

Fruits.

Coffee.

Toast List.

The "King".	Col. C. B. O. Symons, C.M.G., D.S.O., R.E.
The Guest of the Evening.	Col. C. B, O. Symons, C.M.G., D.S.O., R.E.
	Seconded by Mr. D. L. Morgan.
The "Forces".	Proposed by Rev. John Van Ess. Reply by Group Capt. Courtney, C.B.E.
Iraq.	Proposed by Mr. Todd, O.B.E. Reply by Major Wilson.
The Ladies.	Proposed by Capt. Bennett, M.C Reply by Mr. Woodman.

Toast Master : Capt. J. M. Morris.

On the Friday evening I was entertained to a wonderful Farewell Dinner by my officers at the Makina Club. They had also invited all the officers commanding the local Army and RAF units, the heads of Civil Service departments, and principal residents of Basra. There were 48 of us present at the dinner, and on this occasion Colonel C.B. Owen Symons CMG DSO RE, whom I had known since the early days of the War, proposed the toast to me. He mentioned that my duties entailed travelling all over the country and into Persia, and that I knew Mesopotamia from the Garden of Eden to its farthest corner. "When the D.D. of Works, Basra, had handed over to the speaker (Col. Symons) he wrote to say that his assistant (Colonel Lott) was the soundest and most knowledgeable man in the whole of Iraq. What he does not know of the country you will never miss."

In seconding the toast, Mr D L Morgan said that "In stating that Colonel Lott, in this drear and distant land, has upheld the best traditions of an English gentleman, I am merely voicing the opinion of everyone who has come into contact with him. We have all come into contact with his firm, just, and able administration. The ability of a man is gauged by the loyalty and devotion of his officers, and my colleagues will agree and endorse my statement when I say that, if and when they wanted advice and assistance, Colonel Lott was always the first person they would go to."

On that last Friday I received my final pay settlement of Rps.7,174/-, and went to the bank in Ashar to withdraw Rps.5,300/- and remit the balance of Rps.5,474/- (£393) to London. My accounts showed that my total assets when I left in February had risen to £4,170 from a total of £2,320 in September 1921, and I had had a thoroughly interesting and enjoyable time!

And so ended the nine years I had spent in and attached to the Army and Royal Air Force. Since I started in the War by paying my own passage from Montreal to London, via New York, in

December 1914, I was able, by a War Office concession, to claim a free passage back to Montreal. Thus I received a 'voucher' for a first class ticket from Bombay to Montreal, and was able to exchange it, by the payment of only £47 extra, for a ticket by the longer route round the world, instead of going by the Suez Canal, the Mediterranean and Marseilles.

By an extraordinary stroke of luck, I found that the first 'Round the World' luxury cruise ship, the 22,000 tons Empress of Canada, was in Bombay harbour, and had vacancies for a few extra passengers.

I left Basra on the S.S. Vasna on Saturday 23rd February 1924, bound for Bombay. That morning I had collected my medical certificate from Nodwell, completed my packing, and seen my luggage off. Then I had gone round with Henderson, paying calls and saying my goodbyes to everyone. I received a wonderful send-off; practically all my officers and the RAF people turned up, as well as the Chief Engineer. The Rajputs were leaving on the same ship, and their band enlivened the occasion, whilst an aeroplane circled the ship and did some stunts as we set sail.

After a short stop-over in India, during which I travelled by train to Delhi and Agra for my second visit there to explore and photograph, I boarded the Empress of Canada for my return journey to England, seeing more countries on the way than I had thought possible, moreover under much pleasanter conditions and at much less cost, having the advantages of living in a floating luxury hotel, where I could leave my baggage and go ashore for as many days and nights as the ship was in port. The description of the three and a half months of that trip is included in the next volume. I shall close this volume with my favourite Arab proverb:

"I had no shoes and I murmured – until I met a man who had no feet."

Report in The Times of Mesopotamia of my Farewell Dinner at the Makina Club on 22nd February 1924

BANQUET AT MAKINAH

COLONEL H. C. LOTT BIDS FAREWELL TO 'IRAQ.

Makinah Club, February 22.

A large and representative gathering of the service and civil community of Basrah assembled to-night at the farewell dinner organised by the officers of the Works and Building Department of the Royal Air Force in honour of Colonel H. C. Lott M.C., Senior Works Officer of the Basrah District. Formerly in the Royal Engineers, Colonel Lott has served for some eight years in 'Iraq and at one time his district extended to the Caspian Sea.

Colonel Lott like all who know this country well has a profound belief in its development possibilities and his regret on leaving is shared by a host of friends.

His route to Canada will be by way of Japan and China and possibly he will visit the upper reaches of the Yang-tze-Kiang river if the times are propitious.

The guests were drawn from almost every branch of 'Iraq life, including members of the R.A.F. and Military Forces. The Press, Law, Church, Medicine, Commerce, the P. W. D. and the Disposals Board, Local Government and Political Departments the 'Iraq Railways and the leading Bankers of the Station.

Col. Lott, Col. Symons, Group Capt. Courtney, Major Wilson, Dr. Van Ess, Capt. Bennett, Mr. Todd, Mr. Henderson, Wg. Com. Glynn, Dr. Borrie, Mr. Woodman, Capt. Gault Macgowan, Mr. Smith, Mr. Murray, Mr. Cooper Fl. Lt. Bowen, Mr. Inglis, Mr. Harding, Mr. Jennings, Capt. Morris, Mr. Underwood, F/O. O'Connor, F/O. Cleasby, Mr. Fowler, Mr. Bertram, Mr. R. G. Bond, Mr. MacPherson Mr. Blackwood, Mr. Bagot, Major McDonald, Capt. Masters, Major Johnston, Mr. Garbutt, Capt. Greeves, Mr. Roden, Sq. Ld, Havers, Capt. Pulpher, Mr. Phillips, Mr. Morgan, Capt. Parry, Mr. Chamberlain, Capt. Livingstone, Major Mabbett Capt. Bardon, Mr. Thorne. Major Bourne, Major Ovens.

After the Loyal Toast the president Colonel C. B. Owen Symons C.M.G. D.S.O. R.E. rose to propose the guest of the evening, Colonel Lott who had been known to him since the early days of the war. The speaker had thought of writing a set speech in order to do Colonel Lott justice but he had decided instead to say what he knew plainly and without eulogies. Colonel Lott was serving with the 8th Royal Sussex Regiment the Pioneers of the 18th Division when they first met in France .t Thiepval in July 15 a spot both would long remember, for the mud there eclipsed that of Busrah. Colonel then Captain Lott very shortly afterwards transferred to the Royal Engineers much to the regret of his C.O. who whenever faced with a stiff operation bemoaned the absence of his trusty officer. " I wish I had Lott here" he said often to the C.R.E. Captain Lott' progress in the Sappers was rapid. He was a Major in May 1918 and a Colonel in 1919. He was 3 times mentioned in despatches and twice wounded. His duties when he was sent to 'Iraq entailed his travelling all over the country and into Persia. He knew Mesopotamia from the Garden of Eden to its farthest corner.

When the D. D. of Works Basrah handed over to the speaker he wrote to say that his assistant was the soundest and most knowledgeable man in the whole of 'Iraq. "What he does not know about the country you will never miss." Colonel Symons was relieved to hear he would have an experienced officer on his Staff but great was his surprise in landing at Basrah to meet his old friend of the 18th Division. He had further reason since that happy meeting to be more than ever grateful for Colonel Lott's assistance, his technical knowledge and outspoken honesty which had earned the respect of all. He wished him Bon Voyage and good luck in the future.

Report in The Times of Mesopotamia of my Farewell Dinner at the Makina Club on 22nd February 1924 (contd)

Mr. D. L. Morgan seconding the toast said "Col. Symons and Gentlemen, it affords me great pleasure to second the able and appropriate remarks which you, Sir have just made. I do not think there is anyone in the room to-night who has been so closely and for such a length of time associated with Col. Lott as myself. I am sure there is no one here to-night who better appreciates his sterling qualities. I have known Col. Lott for over four years in this country, during which period I have been in continuous close contact with his work and shining personality. The far flung Battle-line of the Empire we are all so proud to belong to, has been sustained by great and able men in many far and distant lands. The base on which their success was firmly built is that they were first and last English Gentlemen without fear and above reproach. When I say that Col. Lott in this drear and distant land has upheld the best traditions of an English Gentleman I am merely voicing the opinion of everyone who has come in contact with him. As Deputy Director of Works now Senior Works Officer Basrah District we have all come in contact with his firm just and able administration. The ability of a man is gauged by the loyalty and devotion of his officers and my colleagues will agree with and endorse my statement when I say, that if and when they wanted advice and assistance Col. Lott was always the first person they would go to.

The Royal Air Force are losing an able Administrator. We are losing not only that but a sincere friend and an elder Brother.

Col. Lott is still a young man, he is only at the beginning of the prime of his life. He has already carved out an honourable name for himself. I am confident that in the many long years of prosperous life before him that he will travel far on the road to success and fame. He has all our good wishes in this direction.

COLONEL LOTT'S REPLY.

Colonel Lott rose to reply opening with his now famous Basrah dictum "Engineers are not good speakers" Much to his regret Colonel Symon's speech had disabused him of that theory. He had asked for no speeches at the banquet. It was the first time his authority had been defied. From the speeches he had heard it seemed he had been a wonderful chief but that was entirely due to his admirable assistants who had supported him through thick and thin A senior works officer was really between the devil and the deep blue sea-the devil being—O. C. units and the deep blue sea-the Chief Engineer (laughter). As a result he had become a very retiring man for if ever he ventured into the Club he was buttonholed by some C.O. who wanted a new dado for his mess or an extension to his polo stable. If he granted the request the chief Engineer groused about the increase in costs. He was bound to be criticised either way. However both had been very kind. He had been very loathe to leave Baghdad but Basrah had proved a welcome surprise. He paid a tribute to Mr. Morgan his assistant who had supported him through difficulties and dangers which help he hoped would be extended to his successor Captain Henderson. He pointed out he was not the only departing guest. The Rajput Regiment were leaving them too and he wished Bon-Voyage to them all represented by Major Johnston and Major Ovens who were present.

127

The formalities ended with a toast to the Forces by
The Rev. Dr. Van Ess

STRIKING SPEECH BY DR. VAN ESS.
a USA Missionar

The Rev. John Van Ess then rose to propose the health of the Forces. He pointed out that on the original toast list he had been asked to propose a toast to the Church with which he could not comply as the Church never toasted but only roasted (laugher). He thought that in proposing the health of Colonel Lott they should "Remember Lot's wife" (laughter). He thought this was perhaps a sentiment for the future (loud and prolonged applause).

He paid a tribute to the work accomplished by the British in 'Iraq with the eyes of the Arab upon them. Despite criticisms of the British administration by the most violent of antagonistic Arabs he had never met an Arab yet and he had been many years in 'Iraq, who had not a good word to say for what had been accomplished by the British.

In a stirring appeal he asked Britains not to forget the past. There were 30,000 British graves in 'Iraq and civilisation had been saved as much at the battle of Shaibah as it had ever been in history. He recounted an incident in the fight when a captain who disobeyed an order to retire and attacked instead with the bayonet turned defeat into victory.

In the name of a common culture which was faced with enormous foreign forces watching British administration with a jealous eye, he asked them to finish the day's work in 'Iraq and not to forget the past.

Office of the Chief Engineer,
British Forces in 'Iraq,

Baghdad, 12 th August 1924.

I have great pleasure in testifying to the excellent work done by Mr. H. C. LOTT as Senior Works Officer at Basra, as a member of the staff of the Works & Buildings department of the Air Ministry in 'Iraq.

He has proved himself a most capable Engineer of wide general experience including Civil, Mechanical and Electrical work.

He has always been a keen, energetic and loyal worker and by his able management of the large Basra area, comprising Power House, Pumping and Filtration installations, Ice Plant, Light Railway and Workshops, as well as Hospital, Stores, and barracks, has rendered me great assistance as Chief Engineer in 'Iraq.

Colonel,
Chief Engineer,
British Forces in 'Iraq.

Col. Symons added a personal letter saying:

"I shall not be sorry when my time is up here. I have tried many parts of the world and am of the opinion that this is the least likeable of all. I hear that Morgan was married last month and there is rumour that Inglis is going to be married when he goes home next spring. So it looks as if Basra air or life rather encouraged matrimony.

I hope that we may meet when I get Home early next summer and have a yarn about old times."

Lightning Source UK Ltd.
Milton Keynes UK
UKHW020852230421
382484UK00006B/157